THE COMIC
BOOK
OF
MI5

BRANDON

First published 1987
Brandon Book Publishers
Dingle, Co Kerry, Ireland

British Library Cataloguing in Publication Data
Fitzgerald, Patrick
The comic book of MI5.
1. MI5 — Anecdotes, facetiae, satire, etc.
I. Title II. Cormac
327.1'2'0941 UB248.G7
ISBN 0 86322 094 0

Cover design: Cormac
Typesetting: Fingerprint
Printed by Richard Clay, England

Introduction

The modern intelligence profession resembles in some respects a mediaeval monastic order. Its members are set apart from the rest of society, bound by vows of secrecy and constrained by the demands of the "need-to-know" principle (under which no one is told more than absolutely necessary about anything). Members of an individual intelligence service share a common code of ethics and customs which helps to east the strain of isolation and to promote a sense of solidarity within the service. To the outsider, these values often seem utterly warped — such as the comment of one MI5 officer that recruiting agents was like breaking someone's leg so that one might offer them a crutch. All these factors breed suspicion towards the outside world, which is quite fairly reciprocated. The profession is one which appeals to the alienated, and not surprisingly it draws a few odd characters within its shroud.

The supreme object of worship for intelligence services generally is the ill-defined concept of "national security". Here the British intelligence services are far less vulnerable to external political control than their counterparts elsewhere in the West. The doctrine of mutual independence and oversight between the three sectors of state power — the executive, the judiciary and the law-making body — has never been properly effective in Britain due to the lack of a written constitution. A simple invocation of "national security" will guarantee the executive a clear run in almost any context. The British intelligence services are further blessed with the vaguest legislative framework it is possible to imagine; to the point where the nation's top civil servant, Sir Robert Armstrong, can sit before a foreign court and simply refuse to admit the existence of a British secret service.

Yet the very lack of any accountability or any counterweight to executive power has recently caused a crisis in British Intelligence, especially the domestic security service, MI5. Neither Peter Wright, representing the manic mole-hunter faction, nor John Lewis Jones, the recently retired Director-General who holds trade unions to be the root of (nearly) all evil, seem wholly familiar with the increasingly complex security landscape. The pleading headline of the *Mail On Sunday* — "Control Us, Say The Spies" — testifies to the self-doubt now afflicting the chieftains of British Intelligence after years of imperial certainties and freedom from meddling by politicians and judges.

The comical aspects of British Intelligence are both personal and institutional. There are four main organisations in the intelligence complex.

The Special Branch operates under the direction of MI5. Each police force has its own separate Special Branch, while the Metropolitan Special Branch has a higher degree of autonomy due to its historical role in countering Irish bombing campaigns in Britain. The Special Branch totals 1,500 officers (including the RUC) and has an annual budget of £40 million.

MI5, the Security Service, operates on UK territory. It's staff of 2,000 subsist on an estimated budget of £170 million. MI5 is divided into:

A Branch — Resources and Technical Operations
B Branch — Personnel
C Branch — Protective Security
F Branch — Domestic Subversion
K Branch — Counter-Espionage
S Branch — Support Services

MI6, the Secret Intelligence Service, operates mainly outside the UK. It has a staff of 3,000 and an estimated £150 million budget.

GCHQ, the Government Communications Headquarters, is responsible for signals intelligence, i.e., the interception and analysis of communications and other electronic signals (such as radar, missile telemetry). It is based in Cheltenham, Gloucestershire, with a worldwide network of eavesdropping stations and a staff of 11,500. Estimated budget, £700 million.

But all of the stories told here are ascribed to particular individuals. The tales are in no sense uniform, either in length, content or era. There are the foibles and idiosyncracies of British spooks; and there are the experiences of those outsiders who, for better or (usually) worse, have crossed paths with the intelligence services — or, as the service coyly puts it, they "come to our attention". And there are illustrations of the absurdities and misunderstandings that invariably arise from the endless convolutions of secrecy, deception and bureaucratic chicanery that characterise the spy trade.

Patrick Fitzgerald
London, October 1987.

Philip ALDRIDGE

During August 1982, Aldridge served in a small section of the Defence Intelligence Staff covering intelligence material from Argentina and the Falklands. The following January he was jailed for four years after stealing a classified document, which he obtained while working there, and trying unsuccessfully to sell it to the Soviets. Aldridge made contact through coded messages entered in the personal columns of the *Daily Telegraph*. Aldridge was "Spider", and the Soviet embassy was "Mum".

Robert ARMSTRONG

Secretary to the Cabinet since 1979 and Head of the Home Civil Service since 1983, Armstrong is Britain's top civil servant and Thatcher's senior adviser on intelligence and security. His background and "high-flyer" progress through the ranks of the civil service were archetypal to the point of caricature. After a classical education at Eton and Christ-church College, Oxford, he joined the Treasury in 1950. Between then and Thatcher's arrival at Downing Street, he worked on the staff of three Prime Ministers and three Chancellors of the Exchequer; and during the mid-1970s he was the Home Office official in charge of day-to-day liaison between the Ministry and MI5. His hobbies — Wagner and the Covent Garden opera — are those of an identikit establishment man. Only his divorce in 1985 and remarriage to Pat Carlow, Harold Wilson's ex-cook, suggest the slightest abberation in the Armstrong persona.

Thatcher's administrations have been constantly plagued by leaks of sensitive information from within Whitehall. Some investigations to find the culprit have been handled in-house by departmental security staff, but Thatcher has increasingly called upon MI5 to make inquiries. Not that they have been conspicuously successful: out of nine inquiries between November 1970 and March 1984, only one was concluded successfully. In the meantime, Armstrong circulated a letter among Whitehall's Permanent Secretaries (the top civil servants attached to each Ministry) urging them to take action to prevent "unauthorised disclosures" in the future. Needless to say, this letter was itself immediately leaked.

Official secrecy and civil service rules of confidence have meant that, despite the importance of their jobs, past Cabinet Secretaries have enjoyed a public profile varying between low and non-existent. Moreover, on those very rare occasions when a Cabinet Secretary has been called before a public hearing in Britain — a court or a Parliamentary committee, for example — they have received the most deferential treatment from their questioners. Robert Armstrong's interrogation in 1986 by the House of Commons committee investigating the Westland affair was fairly tough by normal standards. Although on that occasion he got Thatcher out of trouble with a classic display of the traditional Whitehall arts of obfuscation and semantic legerdemain, it was no preparation for his next public appearance.

When the British decided to seek a court injunction blocking the Australian publication of Peter Wright's tome *Spycatcher*, Armstrong was chosen to be the Government's principal witness. The assignment was turning sour even before he got to Australia. Arriving at Heathrow airport in the middle of November 1986, he discovered a posse of reporters waiting for him; worse still, some of them wanted to take his picture. Sir Robert swung his briefcase at one over-enthusiastic photographer and jostled with others, demanding that his picture should not be taken. He was disappointed on that score but, in a curious exchange later on, he revealed that the briefcase, inscribed in gold with "On Her Majesty's Britannic Service", was no ordinary piece of executive hand-luggage. "Yes, actually, it does have diplomatic immunity," he informed a curious citizen, although it is not clear whether he meant immunity from scrutiny by nosy customs staff or prosecution of the briefcase for assault and criminal damage.

The inauspicious start to the Armstrong mission was a portent of things to come. Sir Robert's chief inquisitor was an ambitious young Australian solicitor named Malcolm Turnbull, who proved to be more than a match for the Cabinet Secretary. Armstrong was repeatedly trapped into admitting inconsistencies and inaccuracies in his oral evidence and in written affidavits previously laid before the court. His tendency to resort to Whitehallesque linguistic contortions only got him into more trouble.

In one exchange, Turnbull probed Armstrong on the contents of a letter Armstrong had written to Sidgwick & Jackson, the publishers of a Chapman Pincher book, *Their Trade Is Treachery*, which revealed information about MI5 mole-hunts. Armstrong had asked the publishers to send him copies of the book. "The only purpose of this request," Armstrong had written, "is to equip the Prime Minister to make a statement . . . . Clearly she cannot do so until she has seen . . . the book itself." Armstrong had neglected to mention in his letter that the Government had already procured a copy of the book (a fact Armstrong had cited in his affidavit) by unspecified means.

Turnbull: "So [the letter] contains a lie?"

Armstrong: "It is a misleading impression. It doesn't contain a lie, I don't think."

Turnbull: "What is the difference between a misleading impression and a lie?"

Armstrong: "A lie is a straight untruth."

Turnbull: "What's a misleading impression, a kind of bent untruth?"

Armstrong: "As one person said, it is perhaps being economical with the truth."

Headline writers couldn't believe their luck. "Economical with the truth" is the phrase for which Armstrong will always be remembered. Worse, as he sadly noted to the judge, "It's not very original, I'm afraid".

A few days later, Sir Robert treated the court to a second, even more bizarre example of Whitehall-think. Turnbull's cross-examination had turned to the foreign espionage organisation, MI6 (also known as SIS, the Secret Intelligence Service). Rather to Turnbull's bemusement, Sir Robert refused to admit the existence of MI6 or any similar organisation engaged in spying overseas. Turnbull reached for the transcripts of the previous day's hearing during which the name of Dick Goldsmith White had cropped up. Turnbull noted that White had been head of MI6 as well as of MI5, and sought confirmation of this fact from the Cabinet Secretary. "He had other jobs," said Armstrong. When Turnbull repeated the question, Armstrong had been more forthcoming: "He was also head of that other organisation". Neither "MI6" nor "SIS" had been spoken, but Armstrong had conceded the existence of "that other organisation". Armstrong wasn't finished though: to the astonishment of the court, he explained that although "that other organisation" (i.e. MI6) had existed when Dick White was head of it, that did not mean that it had existed at any *other* time, before or since.

If the British Government does eventually find an Australian court prepared to grant an injunction, they can take little comfort in having fielded a principal witness who is prepared to utter such inanities in court, apparently in all seriousness. On his return from Sydney, it was business as usual for Sir Robert Armstrong. Yet another threat to national security had emerged in the form of Birmingham City Library. The library holds the diaries of Neville Chamberlain, British Prime Minister at the time of the 1938 Munich crisis, and was seeking permission from the Cabinet Secretary to publish them. Certainly not, replied Armstrong.

Alfred AVISON

Trade union agitator, magistrate, MI5 agent and SAS-trained operative: 51-year-old Alfred Avison is clearly a man to be reckoned with. Demobbed from the Special Air Service in 1956, at the tender age of 20, Avison was already a veteran of anti-terrorist operations in Cyprus, Egypt and the Sinai Desert. "I had to break people's necks, and have strangled terrorists with piano wire," he explained in a graphic interview in 1985 with the *Spalding Guardian*, the local paper in Spalding, Lincolnshire, where Avison lives and works as a "freelance industrial relations consultant" and magistrate. During the 1960s and early 1970s, Avison acquired an impressive reputation as one of the new breed of militants emerging within the middle and lower levels of the old established trade unions like the Transport and General Workers. In 1976, he boasted to the *Daily Mail* of having organised 49 strikes in 18 months. Shortly afterwards, he suddenly switched sides and joined the fruit multinational Geest as an industrial relations adviser. Throughout his career on both sides of the negotiating table, Avison told the *Spalding Guardian*, he was secretly supplying information about trade union activities to a British Intelligence dirty tricks department separate from, but attached to, MI5 and MI6. He later denied doing so, saying that he had been "misunderstood", but refused to comment on another of his claims: that he had given industrial relations advice to Spanish Intelligence during the 1974 Canary Islands strike. It remains unclear whether any of these activities ever actually occurred outside Mr Avison's imagination.

Royd BARKER

Every morning, a battered red bicycle winds its way across London from Notting Hill to a large unmarked office block in Mayfair. Its rider, of late middle age and hawkish features, is Royd Barker, the recently identified head of MI5's A Branch, on his way to work.

Barker's "eccentric" demeanour and "infectious enthusiasm" are entirely apt for his department. A Branch is the place for those who enjoy playing with gadgets and doing naughty things like planting bugs and spiriting confidential records out of social security files. They are guided solely by the Eleventh Commandment: "thou shalt not get caught". The Branch also hosts a group of skilled burglars, known rather absurdly as the "A Team". One MI5 training exercise finds new recruits drawing up plans to break into a house, as one of them explained:

> We were told to come back with a plan of the building. They wanted proper floor plans with the positions of furniture, so we had to sidle up to windows and look in. We had to note how busy the street was, whether the neighbours were there during the day, whether there was a nosy cleaning lady or workman around and where the best escape routes were. Then we took the plans back and they were looked at by the A Team, who told us we were useless and then gave us their version of how to burgle the place.

Barker's name — uniquely among Branch directors — has been kept secret from the civil servants who supervise and liaise with MI5, and who generally prefer to imagine that such things do not go on. Inside MI5, however, Barker is something of a legend. He is also a keen amateur musician and has risen to become conductor of MI5's 100-strong choir whose periodic outings in unmarked vans are intended to inspire camaraderie in the ranks.

Sir Tufton BEAMISH

This delightfully named former Conservative MP is widely assumed to have been the model for Sir Bufton Tufton, the *Private Eye* caricature of an ancient, blimpish Tory from some underpopulated rural backwater. But his shire pedigree and impeccably reactionary views did not exclude him entirely from the attentions of the security machine. During a telephone conversation, some time in the 1950s, with an official in the War Office (now the Ministry of Defence), an anonymous voice broke into the call with the polite but ominous warning: "Please remember that I have been listening to your conversation. Please remember to be more careful in the future."

Cedric BELFRAGE

After disaffected ex-spook Peter *Wright* had first appeared on television in the summer of 1984, Fleet Street's spy experts fell over themselves in the scramble to get the story behind MI5's mad mole-hunt. The weekend after

Wright's small screen debut, the *Sunday Times* uncovered "The List", a roll-call of 21 suspected or proven Soviet agents, supposedly drawn up in part by Wright and categorised according to the alleged degree of their implication. Under a heading called "Partially Confessed" appeared: Cedric Belfrage (film critic, dead).

Although Wright denied the existence of any such list, it appears that the newspaper did hit the mark, barring a few minor details: Belfrage had never confessed to anything, partially or otherwise; he hadn't worked as a film critic since the 1930s; and he wasn't dead.

Mr BELLET

A Home Office civil servant during the late 1930s, Bellet was the recipient of a peculiar letter from a certain Government agency with the strange telegraphic address "Snuffbox". This was, of course, MI5 who were making some rather half-hearted inquiries about the disappearance of a passport belonging to the British fascist leader Oswald Moseley. Although the missive bore huge, prominent stamps with the word SECRET, the letter ended with the following indolent question: "If you are not the proper person to whom this request should be addressed, would you mind passing on this letter?"

Tony BENN

Ex-Labour Cabinet Minister and serious tea-drinker, Benn was the undisputed bogeyman of Britain's conservatives during the 1970s. For the intelligence establishment — never a rich seam of radical thought — Benn's leftist heresies were compounded by his less-than-deferential attitude towards matters of security. As a Minister in the Labour Governments of the 1960s and 1970s, Benn was shocked to discover that Prime Minister Harold Wilson sanctioned routine MI5 surveillance of trade unionists and left-wing activists. Indeed, Wilson "used to boast of the amount of surveillance that he undertook". (Wilson denies boasting — "it is much too serious a subject for doing that".)

Moreover, Benn's own direct, if occasional contacts with the intelligence machine, gave him little confidence in their assessments. His attempt to appoint the transport workers' boss, Jack Jones, to head the National Enterprise Board was blocked: "Box 500 (a cover name for MI5) told me that he was subversive [though] actually, he didn't want the job". Hugh Scanlon, leader of the engineers' union, was similarly blacklisted.

In a different vein, Benn was once invited to meet a delegation from Socialist International, a forum for non-communist social-democratic parties — like the British Labour Party and the German SPD — from all over the world. Benn's Private Secretary, a civil servant, was horrified: under no circumstances, declared the mini-mandarin, could the Minister attend. Whitehall's considered view was that the Socialist International, an organisation boasting such august statesmen as Willi

Brandt and Olof Palme among its patrons, was in fact the same as the tiny Trotskyist group, the International Socialists (now called the Socialist Workers Party).

As Benn reached the zenith of his power towards the end of the 1970s, a cabal of gung-ho right-wing spooks had apparently formed around a leading Tory, Airey Neave MP, to discuss an "army of resistance" to a re-elected Labour Government. Neave, a veteran of wartime intelligence, was one of Margaret Thatcher's closest associates. According to one of the gang, an MI6 contract employee called Harold "Lee" Tracey, they also talked about assassinating Benn if he looked like reaching 10 Downing Street. Such drastic measures proved unnecessary following the decisive Conservative victory of May 1979. Neave, who was expected to take up a dual portfolio as Northern Ireland *gauleiter* and overlord of the intelligence complex, was ironically killed by a car bomb later in the year.

By now, Benn was thoroughly unpopular throughout the intelligence milieu, though even they might have thought a "wet job" to be somewhat excessive. At the end of 1978 he had launched an initiative to commit the Labour Party to future reform of the intelligence services — including the ultimate anathema of parliamentary scrutiny — but the proposals, to Whitehall's great relief, foundered through lack of support. Undeterred, he continued to make public attacks on the security services over the next few years. There is no evidence, however, that they were behind a series of attempted smears during this same period. Richard Ingrams, editor of the satirical fortnightly *Private Eye*, recalls "many anonymous telephone calls in the late 1970s, offering lurid and clearly fantastic stories" about Benn. And in September 1981, as the Benn-Healey struggle for the deputy leader's post came to a climax, a strange letter postmarked Wimbledon from "a disillusioned quizmaster" arrived at the magazine's offices. "What is the connection," it asked, "between

(a) MacFarlane's [a firm of solicitors]; (b) Mr Anthony Benn, candidate; (c) 1979; (d) the Cayman Islands; (e) £3 million?"

The implication was that Benn was involved in a major offshore tax avoidance scheme, which would not have endeared him to his party comrades. *Private Eye* refused the bait. Not so the *Times*, which asserted the existence of a "Stansgate Trust" (Stansgate is Benn's hereditary family title) in Bermuda (rather than the Cayman Islands). The *Times* reporter, Philip Robinson, later conceded that while he lacked proof, he thought that such a trust *might* exist. Benn lost the election nonetheless by the narrowest of margins, and his career as a major political figure went into decline thereafter.

The irony of the Tony Benn saga, as far as British Intelligence is concerned, is that several unsuccessful attempts were made by a "certain colonel" (apparently from MI6) to recruit him as an informer while he was at university and, later on, shortly after he entered Parliament. When Benn revealed this publicly in 1980, he met with much bemusement and some incredulity. The strangest reaction, however, came from the conservative *Times* columnist, Bernard Levin, who confessed that the mysterious "colonel" was none other than himself, using the cover of the Balls Pond Road Ward Section of the Hackney South and Shoreditch Constituency Labour Party. Sadly, added Levin, the potential agent had done no more than make complex queries about pension rights, overtime payments and dismissal procedures, before rebuffing his proposition in a stream of apoplectic diatribe ("hireling lackey of the fascist junta" etc). Intelligence sources suggest that this may have been a rare excursion by the venerable scribe into the field of satirical writing; however, Levin's style is such that this is far from obvious.

Ben BENNETT

In 1984, Ben Bennett revealed startling new evidence to support the theory of Peter Wright and the mole-hunters that ex-MI5 boss Roger Hollis was a Soviet agent. Bennett had been Hollis's regular caddie when the spy chief played golf at his favourite course, Burnham and Berrow, and was thus in a position to observe at close quarters the tell-tale signs that revealed Hollis's true allegiance. "He never sliced a ball. It was always a hooked shot," noted Bennett. "So even in his leisure time he subconsciously favoured the left."

Sigismund Payne BEST

Best's career as one of Britain's better-known spooks began when he signed up for war service in 1915. He was immediately posted to the army Intelligence Corps by virtue of his knowledge of languages and ability to ride a motorcycle, which were then the only qualifications. He rapidly acquired a reputation as competent and inventive: both were rare qualities in British Intelligence at the time, and finding them together was almost unprecedented. In 1916, the British were experiencing severe problems infiltrating agents behind the German lines. Best had a brainwave: why not use balloons? He went off to the Naval Ballooning School to make inquiries. The school's commandant was Commander "Pink Tights" Pollock, a solicitor and veteran pre-war balloonist, whose ludicrous nickname was coined after an airborne mishap in which he lost his trousers and revealed a rather fetching line in underwear. Although Pollock shared Best's enthusiasm for the project, it didn't work out too well in practice. Only three agents were despatched and the resulting information was negligible. Best then suffered another flash of inspiration. Instead of humans, the balloons would carry pigeons.

The British had been using carrier pigeons to carry secure communications since early 1915 and had, much to their initial surprise, found them most effective. Best, Pollock and company built a contraption for releasing the pigeons over German-occupied territory. Attached to each bird was a questionnaire on enemy activities which recipients were encouraged to fill in and send back. Predictably, there were some accidents — such as the balloon-load that landed amongst a squad of hungry Canadian troops and immediately found themselves on the lunch menu — but the operation worked well on the whole. Rumours and legends of pigeonary exploits spread on both sides at every level. At one point, a curious British General was told by Best that a new, superior strain of bird had been produced, by cross-breeding pigeons and parrots, which could fly back *and* report verbally. The General not only took Best seriously but stormed off to headquarters to report him for divulging military secrets.

Back at home, pigeon-power faced a backlash. The unfortunate birds were assumed by the spy-crazed London public to be German agents, ferrying vital secrets back to the Kaiser. Special Branch boss Basil *Thomson* noted that, early in the war,

> it was positively dangerous to be seen in conversation with a pigeon; it was not always safe to be seen in its vicinity. A foreigner walking in one of the parks was actually arrested and sentenced to imprisonment because a pigeon was seen to fly from the place where he was standing and it was assumed that he had liberated it.

After Armistice, Sigismund Payne Best followed the pigeons back into Civvy Street. By 1933 he was a director of a Dutch import-export firm which, when Hitler came to power that year, offered ideal cover for Best's return to the spy business. He was recruited by Claude *Dansey* to work part-time for a semi-autonomous and deeply secret MI6 outfit called the "Z Organisation". His widespread wartime reputation was apt to be an occasional liability, as he discovered on meeting the local MI6 man in the Hague at an embassy reception:

> He welcomed me with shouts of "Hallo, here is old Best the arch spy — I know all about you," etc, etc. The last I saw of him he was vomiting on some lady's lap.

At the beginning of World War II, Best was captured on the Dutch-German frontier by German security during a meeting with bogus anti-Hitler conspirators. He spent the rest of the war incarcerated and may have wished he had stuck to pigeons.

Michael John BETTANEY

Michael Bettaney, the only member of MI5 ever prosecuted for espionage, was born in 1951 in Stoke-on-Trent. In 1969 he began studies at Pembroke College, Oxford, where he built a reputation as an ardent right-winger. After graduation and a couple of years' teaching in Germany, part of it spent living with an Eastern European priest, Bettaney was finally recruited into MI5 in 1975. His active service began in Northern Ireland, where he was stationed for three years — twice as long as the usual posting. The experience was apparently somewhat traumatic and planted the first doubts in his mind about his politics and his work.

Back in London, Bettaney was assigned to a comparatively tedious job in the training department where he became disillusioned and started to drink heavily. In 1981, a colleague lodged a formal complaint after giving him a lift and finding that Bettaney was so drunk he had failed to notice a pall of smoke rising from a lighted pipe lodged inside his pocket. In the autumn of the following year he was found paralytic in London's Oxford Street by police officers who took him off to dry out amid gibbering protestations of "I'm a spy, I'm a spy". The subsequent visit to Marlborough Street magistrates court cost him £12. Eight days later he was back in court again, charged with fare-dodging. Despite these indiscretions, MI5's management still saw fit to move him in 1983 to a key post in the Soviet section of the Counter-Espionage Branch. Perhaps they concurred with Bettaney's subsequent observation that such happenings were not unusual. Indeed, shortly after the Oxford Street incident, another MI5 officer was arrested for urinating in public.

By the time of his transfer, Bettaney's politics had swung from ultra-right to pro-Soviet Marxist. The West, he had decided, was working to destroy the Soviet Union; to help restore the balance, therefore, he would neutralise MI5 operations against the Soviets. His new job gave him access to MI5 reports on Soviet intelligence activities in Britain, the details of which he decided to pass over to the KGB *rezident*. The aim was to establish his bona fides with the Soviets prior to establishing formal contact with them. The KGB, however, failed to respond to his advances. MI5 discovered what he was up to and had him arrested by Special Branch, to whom he made a 180-page confession almost immediately. The Director-General, Sir John Jones, duly reported to the Prime Minister and apparently recommended that there should be no prosecution. Mrs Thatcher, however, had had enough of MI5's back-door solutions and insisted that Bettaney stand trial.

The week-long trial was held in the Old Bailey's No 1 Court during the middle of April 1984. The entire proceedings were conducted in camera, apart from part of the prosecution's opening statement, the verdict and the sentencing. Security measures were severe. The court's windows were boarded up and MI5 technicians made daily sweeps of the courtroom to locate any secreted bugging devices. The jury was thoroughly vetted. The defence lawyers were subject to unprecedented restrictions. Before the trial, relevant official documents were kept in a locked safe and could only be studied in the presence of Special Branch officers; some documents which made up part of the prosecution evidence were forbidden to the defence. At the trial, the defence could not cross-examine Government witnesses on matters concerning "national security"; nor could they call their own expert witnesses. Helena Kennedy, one of Bettaney's lawyers, described the trial as an "absolute farce".

Bettaney was convicted and sentenced to 23 years imprisonment. He was immediately installed in a solitary confinement cell at Coldingley Prison in Surrey with his own personal warder. The section of wall visible from his cell was especially raised to 30 feet to prevent messages from outside. Most important of all, he was supplied with Andrex soft toilet paper — a unique privilege under the British prison system. Security experts recall that Bobby Sands' prison diary was composed on the regular Government-issue hard, shiny stuff: the soft paper is impossible to write on.

KNOW YOUR ENEMY

~ A GUIDE FOR MI5 FIELD OPERATIVES ~

THE BADGE ON THE LAPEL CLEARLY INDICATES THAT THE WEARER IS EITHER

(A) A SOVIET AGENT
OR
(B) A COMMUNIST DUPE

HE MIGHT AS WELL CARRY A BANNER PROCLAIMING ;

" I WANT THE FREE WORLD TO BE ENGULFED BY RED HORDES "

THE WOOLY HAT IS A DEAD GIVEAWAY. THE WOMAN IS OBVIOUSLY A LESBIAN TROTSKYITE VEGETARIAN.

SHE IS CLEARLY PART OF THE INTERNATIONAL CONSPIRACY WHICH AIMS TO SWEEP AWAY PARLIAMENTARY DEMOCRACY, DESTROY THE FAMILY, AND MAKE PRIVATE EDUCATION TERRIBLY EXPENSIVE.

LOOKS QUITE HARMLESS, DOESN'T HE?

BUT DON'T BE TOO SURE!

PERHAPS HE IS A MEMBER OF A **TRADE UNION**,

OR WORSE STILL, A TRADE UNION **ACTIVIST!**

BETTER PUT A TAP ON HIS PHONE — JUST TO BE ON THE SAFE SIDE.

Sean BOURKE

Born in Limerick into an Irish merchant family, Bourke shunned his respectable background and embarked on a career of petty crime. In 1961 he was sentenced to seven years imprisonment for sending a letter bomb to a policeman who had arrested him on a previous occasion. During this stretch, which he served at Wormwood Scrubs in West London, Bourke developed a friendship with George Blake, a former MI6 officer who was jailed, also in 1961, for 42 years for passing secrets to the Soviet Union. In 1966, after his release, Bourke played a central role in organising Blake's escape from prison and travelled with him to Moscow. There is no evidence to support the widespread rumours that Bourke and his British accomplices were financed and controlled by the KGB: indeed, it seems the Russians were as surprised as everyone else when Blake and Bourke turned up.

Bourke stayed in Moscow for two years. He didn't like it and spent much of his time in trying to find a way home. When he eventually got back to Ireland, the British applied for extradition and were rejected; a subsequent MI6 plot to kidnap and smuggle him across the Irish Sea petered out. Bourke spent the rest of his life in Ireland, most of it drinking off the proceeds of his book *The Springing of George Blake*. He died in 1982, aged 49.

The Russians were rather disappointed that Bourke had chosen to embrace socialism and KGB hospitality for only two years. While in Moscow, they had supplied him with a flat, a girlfriend and employment as a translator with a Moscow publishing house. At a preliminary test for this job, Bourke was asked to check a translation of a magazine article describing the life of one Ekaterina Borisovna, a model collective farm manager and leading member of the local Soviet. Bourke was quick to spot a peculiar mistranslation:

> The many-voiced hubbub of a thousand white hens filled the huge barn, their red cocks swaying in the wind.

At the foot of the page he penned the following explanation:

> In English, *cock* is a slang word for the male sexual organ, or penis. Therefore, to talk of hens with their "red cocks swaying in the wind" is to suggest that Ekaterina Borisovna kept some very strange birds. On the other hand, *cock* is also an abbreviation of *cockerel*, the male bird of the species; but it is difficult to imagine why these sturdy creatures should sway in the wind unless, of course, they were drunk. I think the word you are looking for is probably *comb*.

Nigel Cyprian BRIDGE

Better known as Lord Bridge of Harwich and currently one of the five Law Lords. Between 1982 and 1985 he held the post of Judicial Monitor of Interceptions responsible for reviewing the administrative procedures governing phone-tapping and letter-opening (both of which required warrants signed by a Government Minister). In the wake of the Massiter revelations (see Cathy *Massiter*) Bridge was asked by Prime Minister Thatcher to look at all warrants signed between 1970 and 1984 to make sure that each one met the conditions for being properly authorised. Since this was the job which he should have been doing anyway, the appointment of Bridge to conduct the inquiry raised many eyebrows. Even the pro-Government *Daily Telegraph* compared the choice to one of "setting Cerberus to investigate Hell".

Bridge reported, to public astonishment, that not a single one of the 6,129 warrants issued in that period had been improperly authorised. The surprise was not that Bridge had reached this utterly predictable conclusion, but the speed with which he did so — a mere six days after Thatcher's request. Bridge had, according to Home Secretary Leon Brittan, "conducted a full examination of all relevant documents" and considered the merits of each and every warrant. As two of his six days were devoted to other business, Bridge was apparently able to carry out a detailed study of these warrants at a rate of over 1,500 a day. Bridge relinquished his security posts later in the year exhausted, no doubt, by his superhuman effort.

Guy BURGESS

The Soviet agent who worked for the BBC and the Foreign Office before defecting to the Soviet Union with fellow diplomat Donald Maclean in 1951. Burgess was at one stage instructed by his Soviet controller to marry Winston Churchill's niece, Clarissa, to improve his cover. Burgess was horrified. Not only was he a confirmed homosexual, but Clarissa was about as attractive as her uncle.

Nevertheless, he pursued her as requested. There was an unfortunate complication, however, in the form of James Pope-Henessey who had fallen madly in love with her. Pope-Henessey, later a well-known writer, arrived at Burgess' flat one evening and threatened to shoot them both before committing suicide. Clarissa Churchill, unimpressed by both these suitors, instead married Anthony Eden shortly afterwards.

Charles CALLWELL

As the modern British Intelligence apparatus cranked into motion at the turn of the century, Callwell was an early and enthusiastic recruit. He approved especially of collecting intelligence from overseas, and of the Government's newly approved "Secret Service" budget, which enabled the fledgling spies to have "interesting and often very pleasant trips abroad at trifling cost to their own pockets . . . (It was) no small privilege to be enabled to visit at the public expense parts of the world which one otherwise might never have seen." Unhappily, Callwell found that the information acquired was not what it could have been. A particular difficulty was

> dealing with Orientals and savages, whether as informers or spies . . . . The ordinary native found in theatres of war peopled by coloured races lies simply for the love of the thing and his idea of time, number and distance are of the vaguest, even when he is trying to speak the truth.

GLASNOST

What we're talking about here is "sterces"

Sterces is the reverse of secrets...

Sterces is, as it were, palindromic for glasnost...

The trendy demand for more "open-ness" is a threat to our national security!

Oh, well done, Sir! You've just uttered a Margipe!

And what, pray, is a Margipe?

Margipe is palindromic for a turgid little piece of bullshit!

For his services to the British military, if not to race relations, Callwell was later promoted to Major-General and knighted.

Duncan CAMPBELL

"A thoroughly subversive man", was the prosecution counsel's description of journalist Duncan Campbell at one of the most farcical trials of modern times. Campbell, along with another reporter, Crispin Aubrey, had been arrested in February 1977 after visiting John Berry, a former member of the Royal Corps of Signals, to discuss the latter's work on electronic intelligence-gathering. All three were charged under various clauses of the Official Secrets Act and committed for trial in what became known as the ABC trial (after the defendants' surnames).

The accolade from counsel arose from Campbell's previous work for the London magazine *Time Out*, principally a seminal article on GCHQ entitled "The Eavesdroppers", which contributed to the expulsion of Campbell's American co-writer, Mark Hosenball. It brought Campbell to the attention of MI5, who handled the ABC investigation right up to the afternoon of their arrest, and ultimately to the dock of the Old Bailey's No 1 Court.

In 1976, when "The Eavesdroppers" appeared in print, public awareness of GCHQ and its activities was non-existent and should, as far as the Government were concerned, have remained so. Since trade unions at the centre were banned amid vast publicity in 1984, even the most casual punter has acquired a vague notion of what

GCHQ is about; tame espionage author "Nigel *West*" can write a book on the subject and have it approved for publication by Whitehall apparatchiks. Eight years earlier, however, the mere mention of GCHQ was sufficient to put the security establishment into panic mode, especially if someone of Campbell's background was making the inquiries.

The main concern about Campbell was not so much his pro-Labour politics but his considerable technical abilities, particularly in the electronics field. His knowledge and training, which instilled a close attention to detail, enabled him to work out a great deal about GCHQ by analysing information obtained from physical observation and from openly available official and technical publications. The fact that his mother used to work for GCHQ's wartime predecessor, the Government Code and Cypher School at Bletchley Park, no doubt provided additional stimulus for the project. His approach contrasts with that of "traditional" intelligence writers like Chapman Pincher and Nigel West who rely almost totally on closely guarded personal contacts, although obviously Campbell has these too. So when MI5 surveillance picked up on the scheduled meeting with ex-Signal Corps Corporal John Berry, they siezed their chance to get the cuffs on him.

The comedy started from the moment of the arrests. The Special Branch snatch squad had two cars to take the trio to Muswell Hill police station; Aubrey travelled in one; Berry and Campbell in the other. Both cars got lost. One driver eventually found his way after consulting a map; the second couldn't manage even that and had to take directions from a taxi driver. On the following Monday morning, Tottenham magistrates refused bail and had all three remanded in Brixton prison. Yet again, the police got lost on the way, despite the fact that they had

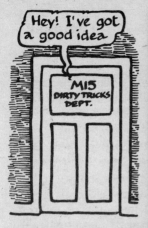

raided Campbell's flat over the weekend and removed a large quantity of documents and books which included three London A-Zs.

At the committal proceedings in November 1977, nine months after the original arrests, the prosecution team introduced their witnesses. So important were they, explained the Crown, and so secret was their work that they could not possibly be identified by name. Taking a cue, perhaps, from the defendants, they were referred to as "Lieutenant-Colonel A", "Colonel B", and "Mr C". Unfortunately for national security, elementary research in the regimental magazines of the Royal Signals revealed "B" to be the head of British army signals intelligence, Colonel Hugh "A" Johnstone. Two magazines which publicly identified him were then prosecuted for contempt and fined.

Almost another year passed before the trial itself opened. The appointed judge, Justice Thesiger, was taken sick and replaced by Justice Willis. The drama began almost immediately on the opening day. Completely by accident, the defence made the stunning discovery that the panel of eighty-odd jurors — from which the final twelve were chosen — had been secretly vetted by Special Branch. Later on, they also discovered that the jury foreman was a former SAS trooper, and asked for his removal on grounds of possible bias (particularly as Campbell had written some less-than-complimentary stuff about the regiment). The judge refused; the trial would continue, and the media would *not* report the dispute about the foreman, under threat of contempt.

The following evening, in the improbable arena of a Russell Harty chat show called "Saturday Night People", the foreman dispute was fleetingly revealed as news which "you won't have read anywhere else". The following

Monday, the court was in pandemonium. Justice Willis and the hapless foreman (who had been watching the programme at the time) were livid. After watching a videotape, Willis said he had no choice but to stop the trial. He recommended prosecution of the television company for contempt but the Labour Attorney-General, Sam Silkin, declined to take up the offer. Silkin had taken most of the flak for the unpopular decision to prosecute the ABC trio, and for the jury vetting revelation; he seemed to be losing heart in the case.

Just as the Special Branch kept getting lost, the ABC judges kept falling ill. Willis went down before the new trial got under way. Justice Mars-Jones took his place. When trial No 2 finally began, Colonel B appeared for the prosecution under his real name. He was asked by defence counsel why he had used "Colonel B" before. "I was told to," he replied sadly. After five days in the witness box, Johnstone, whose main function was to put across the official line on preserving state secrets, had been turned inside out: "To be frank, I'm not certain what is a secret and what isn't". The state's case was in ruins. The charge against Campbell of collecting secret information was humiliatingly dropped after the incriminating evidence, consisting of items such as pictures of the London Post Office Tower, was shown to the court. The prosecution did manage to make the Section 2 charges (communicating and receiving information) stick. None of the defendants were jailed, though some fairly hefty fines were meted out by Mars-Jones, whose health did manage to hold up to the end.

On one occasion during the first trial, Campbell was allowed to leave the court early to give a lecture at the Institute of Physics in Brighton. The topic of his address: British Aspects of Personal Surveillance Devices.

Campbell boasts practical as well as analytical skills in this field. At the time "The Eavesdroppers" was written, Campbell was simultaneously trying to build up his own electronics company in Brighton. He has also developed his own bugging and anti-bugging equipment. One of these devices is the subject of a long-running dispute with his old friends in the Special Branch. On one of the several occasions Special Branch have raided Campbell's home, they removed a blueprint for an infinity transmitter*. So impressed were the spooks that they plagiarised the design. It has never been returned to its originator, nor has he received any compensation.

Perhaps the nastiest encounter between the journalist and the secret police took place in February 1984, when the Special Branch took advantage of an unpleasant accident to raid his house. Campbell is a keen, almost compulsive cyclist. One Thursday, he suffered a serious crash while riding from his workplace at the *New Statesman* magazine to his home in the Stoke Newington district of North London. While he was taken to hospital for treatment, his bicycle and contents of its panniers, including keys and a contacts book, were taken to King's Cross police station. On Saturday morning, shortly before Campbell was discharged from St Bartholomew's, the Special Branch secured a warrant to search his home and, armed with the keys found after the accident, turned up at his house. A group of about 10 officers searched the house for six hours while Campbell, accompanied by editor Hugh Stephenson, looked on. Among the 137 papers which they removed (but later returned) was an appendix to a British army manual. Classified "restricted", it gave vital instructions to squaddies on how to defecate comfortably in a polar environment.

DEEP COVER

I still find it hard to believe....The head of the KGB is none other than Maggie Thatcher!

Only a highly-trained MI5 operative such as myself could have acquired this information....

It's quite amazing what you can learn if you keep your ears open and your mind alert!

Perhaps now she'll tell me what I've always wanted to know....

What do the initials KGB stand for?

*The infinity transmitter is a combined tap and bug. When inserted in a telephone, it is switched on by dialling the number of the target phone and transmitting a specified tone down the line.

Vladimir CHERNOV

In December 1982 Chernov, a Russian translator attached to the International Wheat Organisation, was expelled for "activities incompatible with his position" which in Whitehall-speak means spying. MI5 had decided that Chernov was an officer of the GRU, the Soviet military intelligence service and rival to the KGB. Shortly afterwards, a parcel was delivered to the Gower Street home of MI5's K Branch counter-espionage team, where spirits were high following this victory over the "opposition". Inside was a bottle of rare and expensive Russian vodka and a greetings card on which was scribbled: "Keep up the good work. Best wishes from your friends in the KGB."

Wyndham CHILDS

Appointed at the end of 1921 to take over Special Branch, Childs was a complete contrast in character to his predecessor, the rumbustious, empire-building Basil Thomson. His manner in the face of higher authority was so utterly supine that he became known throughout the

Home Office as "Fido". However, Childs did share Thomson's convictions that the battle against "Bolshevism" was the most important part of the Branch's work and that only the fickleness of the politicians prevented its permanent eradication from the political scene. It was with some misgivings, then, that Childs presented his first weekly intelligence summary to the nation's first Labour Prime Minister, Ramsay MacDonald, in January 1924. MacDonald found the report scarcely more informative than an edition of *Workers' Weekly* and said so to Childs. He also had a few suggestions for "Fido" to chew on:

> [the report] might be made at once more attractive and indeed entertaining if its survey were to cover . . . other political activities of an extreme tendency. For instance a little knowledge in regard to the Fascist movement in this country . . . or the source of the *Morning Post** funds might give an exhilirating flavour to the document and by enlarging its scope convert it into a complete and finished work of art.

Childs was not amused by either this or MacDonald's request, lodged shortly after, to see his Special Branch file. Childs refused, but MacDonald did not pursue the issue.

*Along with the *Daily Mail*, the principal right-wing paper of the day.

Mansfield CUMMING

A larger-than-life character who served as the first head of MI6 between 1909 and 1923, Cumming was renowned for his reckless driving and eccentric treatment of his wooden leg, the legacy of a car accident in France in the opening months of World War I. While interviewing potential recruits to MI6, Cumming would habitually jab at the limb with a penknife or strike matches on it to light his pipe. In the early years of MI6, when it was housed with the War Office, Cumming would race through the building's warren-like corridors with his wooden leg supported by a child's scooter, using his good leg for propulsion. While running MI6 operations during World War I, Cumming enlisted the help of scientists at London University to find an invisible ink for secret messages from his agents. "The best invisible ink," he reported in triumph to a colleague, "is semen". His ambition after retirement was the publication of his unique memoirs:

> I shall call them "The Indiscretions of a Secret Service Chief". It will be a splendid-looking publication bound in red with the title and my name embossed in gold, and consisting of 400 pages — every one of which will be blank.

Claude DANSEY

A prominent figure in MI6 throughout the 1930s and 1940s, Dansey rose to become Assistant Chief of the service during World War II. Born in 1876, the son of a Guards officer, he suffered a relatively traumatic childhood by the standards of the day. He was removed from his school, Wellington College, after an outbreak of diphtheria had killed two fellow pupils, and was sent to an establishment in Belgium where he was bedded by Oscar Wilde's first male lover, Robert Ross. Dansey's schooltime experiences may account for the deep loathing of intellectuals which he displayed in later life. "I have less fear of Bolshies and Fascists than I have of some pedantic but vocal University Professors," he wrote.

After some fun and games in far-flung imperial outposts, he joined MI5 in World War I and found it quite stultifying. Counter-espionage officers thus joined intellectuals among Dansey's pet hates. Dansey then tried his luck in business, met with only moderate success, and in 1929 joined MI6 permanently. Dansey's main achievement of the 1930s was the development of the "Z Organisation", an espionage network which built on Dansey's wide range of business contacts. Dansey, of course, was "Z". He also used a number of other aliases and frequently forgot which one he was using, much to the chagrin of his long-suffering staff. He died in 1947.

Malcolm DEAN

Journalist and security risk. In February 1983, Dean published a series of articles in the *Guardian* based on documents leaked from the Prime Minister's "Family Policy Unit" which was reviewing the Government's social policies. Thatcher called in MI5 to find the culprit. Senior mandarins and civil servants working in Ministers' offices were instructed to fill in a questionnaire with the following penetrating questions:

Do you know Malcolm Dean? — Yes/No.

If "Yes" when did you last meet him?

The inquiry failed to find the leaker and was duly shelved as "inconclusive".

Dean had in fact been positively vetted in 1979, while seconded from the *Guardian* to the Department of Health and Social Security as a special adviser to the Labour Government. The efficiency of MI5 in this field was clear from the timing of his two-hour vetting interview. This took place on 29 March 1979, the day after the Labour Government fell from office, thereby ensuring that Dean and all the other special advisers would have to resign.

Major DENMAN

An old-fashioned military buffer, Denman ran MI5's mail-opening department during the 1950s. This was located on the first floor of the Post Office Special Investigations headquarters near St Paul's Cathedral. On a wall in his office, Denman kept the framed original of a letter sent to a prominent Communist Party member whose mail was regularly opened. The letter read:

To MI5, if you steam this open you are dirty buggers. Denman classed the letter as obscene post and refused to send it on.

Barry DOMVILLE

Between 1927 and 1930, Admiral Sir Barry Domville was Director of Naval Intelligence. Since the Admiralty had ceded control of its wartime code-breaking department to the Foreign Office in 1922, the post had lost some of its prestige. In Domville's case, this was probably just as well. His attitude to intelligence was typified by his complaint of constantly being provided with

> priceless documents from the numerous lunatics who were always paradoxically anxious to help me in collecting intelligence . . . . This type of work appeals apparently to the disordered mind. Not very complimentary, I found it!

Domville might have preferred intelligence work later in life, once his mind was suitably deranged. In the 1930s he became an admirer of Hitler — "absolutely terrific; absolutely A1" — and he set out to uncover "what Masons, Jews and other secret forces at work in our Society were up to". His efforts were to no avail. Domville had got on the wrong side of MI5 long before: come the war, Domville was jailed under the Defence of the Realm Act.

Dermot DUNLOP

"The Security Service does not recruit from Major-Generals" was the reply to Major-General Dermot Dunlop, former General-Officer-Commanding the British forces in Singapore, when he applied to join MI5 in September 1951. However, when it was discovered shortly afterwards that several of HM's diplomatic bags had been broken into while in transit between the colonies and London, the Colonial Office and MI5 decided that an official should be employed on a temporary basis to review security procedures in all British territories. Protocol dictated that this official's seniority should be sufficient to speak to colonial Governors at their own level. Thus was the Major-General's ambition fulfilled, and he served 15 years as a Government security adviser.

Ray FRAWLEY

A sometime member of the planning staff at GCHQ Cheltenham who was despatched to London in the 1950s to liaise with MI5's technical staff, Frawley was a radical atheist who believed that, in the future, mankind would be coupled directly to computers, thereby banishing human irrationality.

Martin FURNIVAL-JONES

A career MI5 officer of markedly patrician manner who rose to become Director-General from 1965 until 1972. Two years into his spell at the top, FJ (as he was known in the office) travelled to Australia to attend a meeting of American, Australian, Canadian and New Zealand spooks. In his passport, against occupation, Furnival-Jones had inserted the absurd entry: "Gentleman". The Australian passport control officer was not impressed. "What's this?" he asked. "That is my occupation," replied Furnival-Jones, "I have no other. I am a gentleman. Don't you have them here?"

Towards the end of his career in MI5, FJ was called to give evidence before the Franks Committee, a high-powered body investigating possible reforms to the Official Secrets Act. Asked what he thought should be considered officially secret, FJ answered with the memorable phrase: "It's an official secret if it's in an official file".

After leaving MI5, FJ's gentlemanly talents were employed as head of security for the Playboy soft-porn empire.

Leopoldo GALTIERI

Leader of the "Argies" during the Falklands/Malvinas conflict of 1982, the whisky-loving Galtieri was one of the targets of a British intelligence operation during the war. The invading Argentinians used a submarine telephone cable for communication between the islands and the mainland. This, they believed, would be less vulnerable to British eavesdropping than the alternative of using radio channels. GCHQ, the British electronic spying organisation, had other ideas. According to one source:

> the British Telecom cable-laying ship *Iris* was especially refitted in Southampton and sent out with the Falklands task force to retrieve a Falklands-Argentina submarine cable from the ocean bed and fit an induction loop tap* to it.

The intercepted traffic from the cable was relayed back to the British Telecom radio station at Portishead near Bristol, where the otherwise smooth operation suffered a bizarre, if temporary breach in security:

> Sensitivity to [the ship's] secret role probably prompted the quick response of GCHQ in reputedly replacing British Telecom staff overnight at Portishead after it was discovered that they were playing Galtieri's phone calls over their public address system.

*A phone-tapping device which works by detecting changes in the magnetic field around the cable.

Anatoly GOLITSIN

Anatoly Golitsin, variously known as Klimov, John Stone, Kago, AE-Ladle, and Martel, is credited in some quarters as having caused more damage to Western counter-intelligence since World War II than Blunt, Philby and George Blake put together. Given that the Ukraine-born Golitsin was one of the most senior KGB officers ever to

defect from the Soviet Union, this is quite a distinction.

One December night in 1961 Golitsin presented himself at the home of the CIA station chief in Helsinki and demanded asylum for himself and his family. His request was granted immediately. Once in the United States, ensconced at the CIA's defectors' hotel at Ashford Farm, Virginia, Golitsin reeled off a vast list of serving KGB officers, current KGB operations and Soviet penetrations of Western intelligence agencies. Golitsin's information was of such high quality that the CIA were more than prepared to accommodate his idiosyncratic and temperamental behaviour. He refused to talk to people he disliked (nearly everybody); he refused to talk to any Russian-speaking officers (they might be moles). Large doses of flattery helped to keep Golitsin sweet: the Americans arranged a meeting with Robert Kennedy; the British wheeled out the gongs and made him a Commander of the British Empire.

The real trouble started when Golitsin came up against the classic defector's problem, namely, what to do when you've run out of stories about your previous employers. Many defectors are quietly pensioned off with a new identity and spend the rest of their lives suffering from paranoia and chronic homesickness. As far as Golitsin was concerned, however, his work had only just begun. The Soviet Union, in his view, had embarked on a geopolitical strategy of breathtaking scale and complexity, in which penetration of the West's intelligence services was only a preliminary stage. The main part of the KGB plan, according to Golitsin, was to use these same "moles" to sow disinformation about Soviet intentions so as to leave Western Governments stupified and helpless to confront the international communist conspiracy.

Golitsin

Golitsin told his Western hosts that, although he was unable to identify these "moles" immediately, if he had free access to their files, his own special "methodology" would uncover them. There was widespread outrage at the idea of allowing a defector, however important, to run around the precious registries of the CIA and MI5, but "Golliwog" (MI5's pet name for him) boasted an influential fan-club, including James Angleton, the CIA's powerful head of counter-intelligence, and the MI5 mole-hunters Arthur Martin and Peter Wright. Their obsessive pursuit of supposed Soviet agents within their own ranks — aptly dubbed "molaria" by one writer — came close to reducing both services to near-paralysis.

Wright later became disillusioned with "Golliwog" on experiencing his much-vaunted "methodology" at firsthand. Examining some decoded KGB cypher traffic at MI5 headquarters, became particularly interested in two likely agents codenamed DAVID and ROSA. After several days deliberation, he announced triumphantly to Peter Wright: "Your spies are here. My methodology has uncovered them".

Golitsin was pointing at two files on the table before him. They belonged to Victor Rothschild, of the eponymous banking family, and his wife Tess. Rothschild was an intimate of cabinet ministers, mandarins and money men and a formidable power-broker in his own right. He was also a former MI5 officer and retained close links with the agency, not least with Peter Wright, who told Golitsin not to make such absurd allegations.

"How on earth did you jump at that conclusion?" asked Wright.

"They are Jewish. David and Rosa are Jewish names," replied the methodologist.

Golitsin

Not surprisingly, Golitsin's star waned in the 1970s with the demise, retirement or disillusionment of most of his supporters in Britain and America. In 1984, with the help of a clutch of loyal fans, he published his memoirs. The book, *New Lies For Old*, published in 1984, is a mind-boggling exposition of Golitsin's disinformation theories which, if even partially true, would demand a complete rewrite of late 20th century history. Among his allegations:

The acrimonious split in 1960 between the Soviet Union and China was phoney; so were the Soviet splits with Albania and Yugoslavia. The idea was to make the West believe that the communist world was fraught with internal divisions, when in reality it was firmly united.

Dissident and reformist movements in the Soviet bloc are illusions. Sakharov is a secret KGB agent; so was Dubcek. Solidarnosc was created and controlled by Soviet Intelligence.

Golitsin's authenticity as a defector has never been doubted. He cleverly covered his back by declaring that other defectors would arrive after him and contradict his assertions — as indeed they did — but that these defectors were in fact fraudulent. But is it possible that Golitsin himself was a KGB plant? Did he merely reveal genuine KGB operations to establish his credentials? Was his real assignment to create total confusion within Western intelligence, in which he succeeded admirably?

"It is useful to compare Golitsin's thesis to, say, the theory of relativity which was, in its day, a revolutionary theory," claimed Stephen de Mowbray, ex-MI6 and one of Golliwog's cheerleaders. Albert Einstein would turn in his grave.

John Irving GOOD

One of GCHQ's premier post-war cryptographers, Jack Good was also a fellow of the Royal Statistical Society and a prolific writer on mathematical topics. Although much of his published work was of high quality, a good deal was somewhat insubstantial. During one temporary hiatus in Good's output, a counterpart at the American National Security Agency had asked a colleague what had become of him and got the reply: "It's an ill Good that blows no wind".

Betty GORDON

In June 1949, Betty Gordon worked in the filing department of a small London publishing firm. The job was tedious: she wanted a change. A vague but intriguing advertisement then appeared in the *Times* seeking "girls of good education" with secretarial skills and even held out the enticing promise of "service abroad". Betty applied and was summoned to an interview with a "Mr MacDonald", who asked a great deal of questions but refused to describe the job. At a second interview, a week later, he was more forthcoming: there was very little money; the job was risky; she might lose all her friends; she could even end up in a mental hospital. As if these incentives were not enough, "MacDonald" — a false name — played his trump card: "You'll be working for your King and Country". Suitably impressed, Betty signed up to join MI5. She didn't quite know what MI5 did, but it all seemed very exciting.

Betty Gordon's assignment was to infiltrate the Communist Party of Great Britain, in line with instructions to MI5 from the Labour Prime Minister Clement Attlee asking for increased surveillance of communists. After grafting as an ordinary party member for a while, Gordon landed a job with the journal *Soviet Weekly*. Although she was a trusted agent by now, MI5 kept an eye on her:

> I met this Arabist academic in the park and fell in love with him. Whilst I was with him, MI5 rang and said, "You've got someone in bed with you". I told them: "That's none of your business". They said: "He's married" . . . . It was true.

When she later got pregnant by him, however, MI5 were well pleased. "They could still use me with a baby. They said a baby was good cover." In 1958, Gordon acquired a job in East Berlin on an English-language paper produced by the International Women's Federation. Periodically she was required to make the risky journey to the Western part of the city at night, leaving her infant behind, to meet her MI5 contact who frequently didn't turn up. Two years later, despite MI5 entreaties, she gave up spying because of the strain. As "MacDonald" had speculated, she later had a nervous breakdown, and spent a brief spell in prison. In 1974, a decade and a half later, MI5 optimistically tried to re-enlist her while she was working for the enrolment department at Chelsea Art College. Service to Queen and Country seemed less alluring on this occasion, and she declined.

JUST BECAUSE YOU'RE PARANOID....

...DOESN'T MEAN THAT WE'RE NOT TAPPING YOUR PHONE.

JUST BECAUSE THEY REALLY ARE OUT TO GET YOU DOESN'T MEAN THAT YOU'RE NOT PARANOID...

Richard GOTT

In 1981, Gott was chosen to edit the BBC magazine *The Listener*. He had previously worked as a foreign correspondent in Latin America, where he fell foul of the Bolivian regime who arrested him for "communism". His BBC appointment was blocked, however, when his file was sent off for "colleging" — vetting by MI5. "They said he was an ultra-leftist," admits a BBC executive. "The phrase was: 'He digs with the wrong foot'."

Stuart HAMPSHIRE

The Labour Government that took office in 1964 was worried about the escalating cost of the GCHQ electronic eavesdropping empire, which had just topped £100 million per annum. (The figure today is around £700 million.) Prime Minister Wilson asked his Cabinet Secretary, the exquisitely named Burke Trend, to carry out a review. Trend called in Stuart Hampshire, an alumnus of the wartime code-breaking establishment who had subsequently made a career in academia. Hampshire's inquiry took the best part of a year, during which he had unrestricted access to GCHQ plus a six-week-long visit to GCHQ's big brother, the American National Security Agency.

Meanwhile the mole-hunters at MI5 were chasing an old lead in their search for the purported fifth and final member of the Cambridge spy ring (Burgess, Maclean, Philby and Blunt had already been uncovered). Shortly after Burgess fled to Moscow in 1951, an old friend of his called Goronwy Rees had told MI5 that he knew Burgess was a Russian agent. Not only that, but Rees claimed to know of three other "moles" in British Intelligence, one of whom was . . . Stuart Hampshire.

MI5 checked their records. Hampshire had not been vetted before starting his ultra-sensitive GCHQ inquiry. Instead, the MI6 chief Dick White, who had known Hampshire for years, wrote a letter to MI5 vouching for Hampshire's integrity. The letter was filed and that was that. Moreover, Hampshire turned out also to be a sometime friend of Burgess. Although MI5 found no evidence that Hampshire did work for the Russians, there was still a major problem: what would the Americans do if they found out that the man engaged in a comprehensive review of Western signals intelligence was simultaneously under investigation as a Soviet agent, and hadn't even been vetted. The MI5 investigation was quietly buried, until its revelation in the press in the summer of 1984. As expected, the Americans were not pleased.

Judith HART

One of the most difficult aspects of MI5's work is distinguishing between different people who share the same surname. In July 1974, the head of MI5, Michael Hanley, told Prime Minister Harold Wilson that the agency had "documentary evidence" proving that Judith Hart, recently appointed Minister for Overseas Development, had attended a communist convention in Eastern Europe during the 1950s. The "evidence" was a dog-eared 1950 newspaper clipping from the *Daily Worker** showing a photograph of a woman laying a "wreath for peace" at a memorial in Sheffield before joining a Communist Party delegation on a visit to Warsaw. The caption identified her as Mrs *Tudor* Hart, the wife of the leading communist Dr Tudor Hart, but MI5's registry clerks filed it under Mrs *Judith* Hart. As well as informing Wilson, MI5 also leaked the "evidence" to the ultra-right Tory MP Iain "Deep" Sproat to feed his obsession with far-left infiltration of the Labour Party.

By the time of Hanley's approach to Wilson, Mrs Tudor Hart — a South African christened Joyce — had been out of the Communist Party for nearly 20 years and had divorced her husband. She even claimed to vote Conservative. Just to confuse MI5 still further, there was yet another left-wing female Hart, called Jenifer, who was married to Herbert Hart, an academic and ex-MI5 officer. Jenifer Hart was both a Communist Party member and a Soviet agent, who worked during the 1930s in the secret Home Office department which processed warrants for telephone taps and mail checks. In the mid-1960s she was interviewed about her past by the MI5 mole-hunter Peter Wright, who didn't take to her:

> Jenifer Hart was a fussy middle-class woman, too old, I thought, for the fashionably short skirt and white net stockings she was wearing. She told her story quite straightforwardly, but had a condescending, disapproving manner, as if she equated my interest in the left-wing politics of the 1930s with looking up ladies' skirts.

* The Communist Party daily, since renamed the *Morning Star*

Sir Michael HAVERS

During his tenure as Attorney-General under Prime Minister Thatcher, Havers had to cope with more than the normal quantity of security related business (not least the Peter *Wright* case). For their part, MI5 seem to consider Havers to be indiscreet and consequently a security risk. Lunching and pursuing amicable correspondence with arch-subversive Duncan *Campbell* during the latter's *Secret Society* investigations can scarcely have improved his standing in this respect. During the trial of Michael *Bettaney*, some prosecution documents were witheld from Havers even though he was officially leading the prosecution case. In the event, he made little contribution to that trial beyond making an opening statement. Sidekick Kenneth Robinson carried most of the load while Havers was noticeably absent. The trial judge made acid reference in summing-up to his "fleeting appearance" while playful lawyers passed a note to each other reading:

Question: Where is the Attorney-General?
Answer: The whereabouts of the Attorney-General are highly secret. So secret that not even he knows where he is.

Isabel HILTON

Now the Latin American editor of the *Independent*, Hilton missed out on a career in television through the intervention of MI5. During the secret vetting procedure for BBC recruits (see Ronnie *Stoneham*), MI5 had "discovered" Hilton was an organiser of an allegedly pro-Chinese group called the Society for Anglo-Chinese Understanding. She was no such thing. MI5 had confused this organisation with the Scottish-China Association, an academic outfit based at Edinburgh University for whom she helped out as a translator. She didn't take the BBC job anyway but moved to the *Sunday Times*, where she was working when the BBC vetting saga was broken by the *Observer* in 1985. After the *Observer* had contacted her for comment, Hilton immediately got in touch with her own paper but got short shrift from the *Sunday Times* creature who took the call. "Rubbish. That sort of thing doesn't happen in this country," he said. One person who was persuaded by the story, however, was the spook-obsessed MP, Tam Dalyell, who had previously been under the impression that Hilton actually worked for MI5. He later collared her at a television festival to convey his apologies. "I had it on the highest authority from South America," he explained.

James HOGG

In the summer of 1980 a seven-point memorandum from Dumfries and Galloway police, discussing the political activities of an obscure Scottish trade unionist, somehow found its way to the offices of the London weekly magazine *Time Out*. Its intended destination was a mysterious Post Office box in the capital: Director-General, Box 500, Parliament Street BO, London SW1P 1XH.

The memo, stamped with the logo SECRET, was a report

from the local police Special Branch to the headquarters of MI5, which uses "Box 500" as a cover address. The subject of the report was one James Campbell Hogg (NI No WA 79 33 63 D), a shop steward at the Carnation Foods factory in Dumfries. The report, based on unsubstantiated gossip from a "management contact", described Hogg as being "connected with the Socialist Workers Party" whilst referring to his "involvement with the Communist Party of Great Britain". A rudimentary knowledge of left-wing politics would discount simultaneous involvement with the Trotskyist Socialist Workers Party and the Communist Party. Apart from which, Hogg had no connection with either.

Leonard HOOPER

Leonard "Joe" Hooper was one of the leading figures in the post-war British intelligence complex. The bulk of his career was spent at GCHQ, to where he was transferred in 1942 after joining the Air Ministry. In 1952 he was appointed an assistant director, and twelve years later succeeded Clive Loehnis as Director of the Cheltenham-based eavesdropping empire. Loehnis was also referred to as "Joe", prompting erroneous speculation that, just as the head of the British secret service is known as "C", the head of GCHQ is called "Joe": in fact, when Hooper left GCHQ in 1973 his successor was Arthur "Bill" Bonsall. Hooper ended his career as Intelligence Co-ordinator in the Cabinet Office.

By the time Hooper reached the top of GCHQ, it was substantially the largest and most important of the British secret agencies. Moreover, the development of satellites in the early 1960s was set to give a massive boost to international telecommunications — the raw material on which GCHQ eavesdrops to produce its intelligence. (Today, around half of all international communications are transmitted via satellite.) The problem for Hooper and GCHQ was how to get access to the phone calls and telex messages carried by the new medium. In 1967, GCHQ decided to build their own satellite ground station to pick up the traffic. A site was found at Bude in Cornwall, courtesy of the Ministry of Defence and conveniently close to the Post Office ground station at Goonhilly Down, which was already sending phone calls via satellite across the Atlantic. Hooper then hit a snag. The projected cost of the Morwenstow installation, comprising two 100-foot diameter parabolic dishes and associated control equipment, was £500,000. When the Treasury and the Labour Government then in office baulked at the figure and queried the necessity of the project, Hooper resorted to a favourite GCHQ lobbying tactic.

GCHQ has an extremely close relationship with its much larger American counterpart, the National Security Agency (NSA) — so close that GCHQ might fairly be seen as the British subsidiary of a giant, American-dominated intelligence multinational. American pressure on the British Government ensured that Hooper got his way. In 1972, the year before Hooper left GCHQ, the Bude station began its eavesdropping operations. A letter of gratitude from Hooper to NSA boss Pat Carter on the latter's retirement was recently unearthed by the American writer James Bamford. The gushing, confessional tone is quite embarrassing:

> I know that I have leaned shamefully on you, and
> sometimes taken your name in vain, when I needed
> approval for something at this end . . . . The aerials at
> Bude ought to be christened "Pat" and "Louis" [after
> Carter's deputy, Louis Tordella] . . . . I have often felt
> closer to you than to most of my own staff . . . and
> that is something I shall remember and cherish . . . .
> As you can understand, I am pretty apprehensive about
> your successor, and whether I can strike up any kind
> of similar understanding with him. He is a completely
> unknown quantity to all of us. Put in a word for me.

The letter ends with a bizarre piece of bed-chamber
imagery:

> Between us we have ensured that the blankets and
> sheets are more tightly tucked around the bed in which
> our two sets of people lie and, like you, I like it that way.

It remains to be seen whether the intimacy has survived
into the age of the duvet.

John Lawrence IMRIE

Imrie was a senior officer in the recruitment section of MI5's Personnel Branch until his untimely appearance before Horseferry Road magistrates court in April 1979. The charge, to which Imrie pleaded not guilty, was of behaving in an indecent manner contrary to a British Rail by-law. The court heard that, one evening in October 1978, Imrie was observed masturbating in the public lavatories at Victoria station. After a transport police operation lasting half-an-hour, Imrie was arrested at 11.25 pm. In his defence, Imrie claimed that he suffered from a weak bladder and, after a hard night's drinking, was concerned at being caught short on the 11.10 pm to Sydenham. The magistrate was unconvinced by this explanation, particularly as the said train had departed 15 minutes before his arrest, and gave Imrie a conditional discharge with £50 costs.

Maurice JEFFES

Director of Passport Control during World War II. As the official responsible for the issue of visas, Jeffes frequently liaised with MI5 and SIS. He was also the victim of an unusual medical error. A doctor had given him an injection to innoculate against some disease but had used the wrong serum. As a result Jeffes's face had turned a strange purplish blue, not unlike gun metal. Worse, the process was apparently irreversible. This caused the poor Jeffes a certain amount of angst, quite apart from being referred to thereafter as "a colourless administrator". On one occasion in Washington, arriving at an hotel which operated a colour-bar, the management tried to cancel his booking on the grounds that he was coloured.

Anthony JONES

A London-based barrister who gave unofficial legal advice to a variety of left-wing causes during the late 1970s and early 1980s. These included defence campaigns for: Aubrey, Berry and Campbell, tried in 1978 under the Official Secrets Act; Astrid Proll, deported for alleged bombing offences in West Germany; the investigative magazine *The Leveller*, prosecuted for contempt; and the anarchist bookshop in Brixton's Railton Road, which faced eviction by Lambeth Council. In 1984, the magazine *City Limits* confronted Jones with accusations that he was supplying information to MI5, including photographs of activists. Jones denied passing photos, but admitted that he had met MI6 boss Maurice Oldfield in 1978 and various "odd people" over the years who had "picked his brains". At the end of the interview, he said he would "just have to live with it" and repeatedly exclaimed, "Don't trust me, don't trust me!" If Jones was working for MI5, they seem to have engaged in some untypically subtle double-think. As the magazine commented:

Many of the people he came into contact with were

initially suspicious because of his upper-class manner, his pin-striped three-piece suits and his slightly eccentric air. But the reasoning ran that no one wanting to infiltrate left groups would present himself as such an establishment figure.

John Lewis JONES

A miner's son, educated in Wales and at Christ's College, Cambridge, Jones joined MI5 in the mid-1950s as an officer in the Overseas Branch, dealing with security and intelligence in the then substantial portfolio of British colonies. After a spell as MI5 liaison officer in Hong Kong Jones returned to London to join the struggle against subversion and, fittingly, to marry a typist in the department transcribing telephone taps. Later on, in the early 1970s, as head of F Branch (Domestic Subversion) under Michael Hanley, Jones enthusiastically supported the latter's emphasis on surveillance of the "far and wide left" at the expense of traditional counter-espionage. He wanted a substantial increase in the use of "technical resources" — i.e. phone-tapping, bugging and letter-opening — against the dangerous lefties. The principal reason for this, according to ex-MI5 man Peter Wright, was that Jones "could not infiltrate his officers into these left-wing groups since many of them led promiscuous lives, and there were some sacrifices even an MI5 officer would not make for his country".

In 1976 Jones was appointed Deputy Director-General, and then, five years later, Director-General. During his tenure in the top job, Jones attended an MI5-sponsored seminar, held in a large house in the Home Counties, on how the service could improve its public image. A prominent media personage was invited to address the assembled spooks. However, after hearing Jones hold forth on the dangers posed by trade unions and the "threat within", their guest seems to have despaired of doing anything to enhance the public esteem of the much-maligned security service.

After several security scandals, notably those involving Bettaney and Massiter, Jones was retired in 1985 and replaced by the veteran mandarin-diplomat, Anthony Duff.

Andrew KNIGHT

Many people who have strange experiences with their telephones assume that they are being tapped. Clicks, buzzes, extraneous voices and so on are regularly cited as evidence of official eavesdropping. However, with very few exceptions, that sort of interference has nothing to do with tapping: one of the things engineers do before fitting a tap is to clean up the "squeaks and farts" on the line which are characteristic of the antiquated British telephone system. Another, rather different phenomenon which is widely thought to indicate a tap is the "playback". Typically, the victim has just finished a call but, before putting the receiver down, is treated to a recording of the conversation which she or he has just held. A properly installed tap should not produce such an effect: a more

likely sinister explanation is that it is being done deliberately as a form of harassment (the South African security police are particularly fond of it). Yet innocent explanations for the "playback" do exist, as the prominent journalist Andrew Knight once discovered to his embarrassment.

In the autumn of 1978 Knight was editor of the high-brow weekly magazine the *Economist*, a prestigious appointment which regularly brought Knight into contact with the rich and powerful. Knight and his wife had engaged a chef to cook for their auspicious house-guests. One day, Mrs Knight and the chef, an Italian named Paulo Ribero, were discussing a dinner menu over a poor telephone line. After hearing several clicking noises, she suggested they put their phones down and start again. Several attempts to get through produced crossed lines or silence. Finally, to her astonishment, Mrs Knight found herself listening to a recording of the earlier conversation with the chef.

Hubby was informed and shortly afterwards wrote an outraged editorial in his magazine. His phone was being tapped, Knight declared, because of the illustrious company he entertained over dinner, such as ex-Prime Minister Edward Heath, Labour Party big-wig Denis Healey and the Governor of the Bank of England. The Post Office, moving with unusual alacrity, replaced the Knight's telephone as well as their chef's set.

The true explanation emerged a few days later. The culprit was a Mr James Hazan of Maida Vale, a long-suffering Post Office telephone subscriber constantly afflicted by crossed lines:

> The other night I picked up the telephone and heard a woman talking to a chef about cookery. I am very

interested in cookery, so instead of hanging up, or asking them to get off the line, I listened . . . it is my hobby, and the recipe sounded good. I tape-record all my own conversations because I have a very bad memory, so I connected the telephone to my tape machine.

Unfortunately he neglected to put the phone back on the hook before playing back the recording of the recipe, which is what Mrs Knight heard when she re—dialled into the same crossed line. Hazan was apologetic to the Knights, but more bitter than ever about the Post Office.

I never meant to cause such a fuss, and I will be getting in touch with the Post Office. But I am furious that Mr Ribero, the chef, has got a new telephone because of all the fuss and I, who have been complaining for so long, have been ignored.

Pamela LAMBLE

Pamela Lamble's quarter-century career as a confidential secretary with the Ministry of Defence and the foreign intelligence service, MI6, came to a strange end in the closing months of 1978.

Lamble had, it seems, become concerned over lapses in security procedures at Century House, the MI6 headquarters where she worked. Repeated efforts to convince her superiors were dismissed as "eccentric" and, in time-honoured security service fashion, she was sent to see a psychiatrist. In September 1978, without returning from

"sick leave", she left her job and hatched a devious plot to vent her fears to a wider audience. The following month, she apparently wrote a letter outlining her critique of MI6 security to an unidentified Soviet bloc embassy. The letter was intercepted by MI5 who promptly sent Special Branch sleuths after her. In the week that the Anthony Blunt "Fourth Man" scandal hit the headlines, Lamble was arrested at her home in Staines, near London, and charged under the Official Secrets Act. After four weeks on remand in Holloway Prison, she was brought before Bow magistrates on Christmas Eve. By that time, the Government had decided that it did not, after all, want to launch a prosecution. Lamble was discharged and ate Christmas dinner at home with mother and a Special Branch minder.

The decision to drop the charges was supposedly taken after Lamble had explained to her interrogators that she *knew* that the letter would be intercepted and that, faced with an ex-MI6 secretary corresponding with the other side, MI5 would actually do something — if only to stick one over on their rivals in MI6. Having swallowed this explanation, the security authorities ordered the inevitable "top secret investigation" while the Attorney-General, Sir Michael Havers, told the bemused press that "after exhaustive inquiries" he was "satisfied that Miss Lamble did not intend to act in a manner which could harm the state". He denied any connection with the Blunt affair, then at its height. Cynics pointed to the potentially embarrassing inconsistency between, on one hand, the immunity granted to the eminent traitor Sir Anthony Blunt and, on the other, the prosecution of a humble secretary motivated only by a patriotic concern for the nation's secrets.

After her release, Lamble said: "I have no idea why they wanted me. I had done nothing wrong that I know of" — an odd and intriguing comment which brought this bizarre episode to a close.

Donald LANCASTER

During the 1950s, Lancaster was an MI6 officer serving under diplomatic cover in South-East Asia. A potential agent (male), passed on by Maurice *Oldfield*, recalls Lancaster's recruiting attempt:

> He invited me to dinner, dismissed the manservant afterwards, and then put his hand on my thigh. I got up and left, and decided not to become a spy . . .

Major-General MASON-MACFARLANE

As Director of Military Intelligence under Field-Marshall Gort during World War II, "Mason-Mac" held his commander in a certain amount of contempt. This was not surprising, going by an incident when Gort stuck his head round the door to ask:

> "Bulgarians? Good chaps, aren't they?"
>
> "No, sir, not terribly good," replied Mason-MacFarlane.
>
> "Oh. Bad chaps, eh? Pity, pity."

Not that Mason-Mac himself was not prone to occasional idiocy, as illustrated by a scheme he dreamt up early in 1940 for dealing with British expatriate pacifists based in Paris:

> Right, I'll tell you what we'll do . . . We'll go down to Paris and kidnap two or three of these charmers. We'll drive them out to the Bois de Boulogne, strip them and let them make their way back to Paris as best they can. At the same time we'll put about a story in the

right places explaining why these people have been dealt with in this fashion.

Much to the relief of his junior staff, the implementation of the plan was inconveniently disrupted by the German invasion of France.

Cathy MASSITER

An MI5 officer between 1970 and 1984, most of whose career was spent in F Branch monitoring "domestic subversion". She was also the star witness in the Channel 4 programme "MI5's Official Secrets" broadcast in March 1985. Along with an anonymous ex-clerk who transcribed intercepted phone calls, Massiter described how MI5 maintained surveillance of trade unions and pressure groups, notably CND, using phone taps and agents infiltrated into the organisations concerned. In the case of CND, moreover, the information obtained was used by Government Ministers campaigning against CND. Massiter became concerned that the CND operation, which she was in charge of between 1981 and 1984, breached the terms of the Maxwell-Fyfe Directive (the nearest thing MI5 has to a rule book) regarding political bias. When she raised the matter with her superiors, they sent her off to see a psychiatrist. She resigned shortly afterwards. "She suffered from the profound disadvantage for an MI5 operative of thinking about her work," commented a former colleague.

Michael McCAUL

In the late 1950s, a technician at a Royal Ordnance factory informed MI5 that he had been approached by a KGB officer and asked for a sample of a new shell which the factory was producing. Michael McCaul, a leading light in counter-espionage, instructed the technician to go to the scheduled meeting with the Russian and arranged for him to take along a dummy shell filled with sand. Both men duly turned up for the rendezvous in a South London park. As the dummy shell exchanged hands, McCaul leapt from the bushes to confront the KGB man and immediately regaled him with a blood-curdling (though fictitious) account of torture in secret MI5 dungeons. The terrified Russian, who realised that he faced expulsion at the very least, began to shake uncontrollably. "Don't drop the shell, for Christ's sake," shrieked McCaul, "you'll trigger the fuse!" The terrified Russian did just that before sprinting from the park. He left Britain the next day.

McCaul subsequently paid a visit to the KGB *rezident* at the Soviet embassy to complain about an approach to one of MI5's surveillance staff. Over tea, the Russian expressed surprise that any of his staff would be so indelicate as to spy on foreign territory but agreed to look into it. "Perhaps the British security authorities have made a mistake," he suggested. "The business has become so crowded these days. So many countries, so many embassies, so many diplomats. Sometimes it is difficult to be sure who is working for whom."

Since you ask, I'll tell you —
Well, I'd like to tell you····

But, you understand, this kind of information is covered by the Official Secrets Act···

Well, of course I'm in favour of freedom of information! I'm not some kind of reactionary dinosaur!

But I did sign the Official Secrets Act. It's a question of trust as well as legality···

There's no need to be quite so hostile and agressive —

All right! All right! If you must know! When I was a clerk in the Ministry of Agriculture I used to take a tea-break at eleven o'clock!

John McWILLIAM

During the parliamentary debate in the spring of 1985 over the Interception of Communications Bill, McWilliam was one of the most important contributors from the opposition benches. As a former telephone engineer sponsored by the British Telecom engineers' union, he knew more than anyone else in the House about the mechanics of phone-tapping. McWilliam was particularly unimpressed with the proposal to establish a tribunal, composed of eminent lawyers, to consider complaints from members of the public that their phones had been improperly tapped.

> I make no complaint about the legal profession. I would not think to lecture the Home Secretary [Leon Brittan] on the legal profession because he is a lawyer and I am not. However, I take it ill when he lectures me about the telephone system and how to intercept it .... I do not believe that the Home Secretary would recognise a bug if it jumped up and bit him, any more than I would recognise a tort if it had jam on it and I thought I could eat it.

Austin MITCHELL

Ex-television presenter and now the Labour MP for Grimsby, Mitchell recently made the novel and probably accurate observation that "in some political circles it is a demonstration of virility to have one's phone tapped".

Graham MITCHELL

From 1956 to 1963, Mitchell was MI5's Deputy Director-General. He was previously head of both the Political Parties Branch, dealing with communists and fascists, and the Counter-Espionage Branch. He was also a compulsive user of toothpicks, which he deployed every day in the office before lunch, after lunch, and before leaving work in the evening. Peter Wright, who investigated Mitchell as a possible Soviet agent, watched him at work with his implement through a one-way mirror. "By the end of the case, I began to feel that the only parts of Mitchell we knew well were his tonsils," he commented.

Malcolm MUGGERIDGE

Author and journalist, Muggeridge served in MI6 during World War II. The irreverent Muggeridge found it more difficult than most to take the spy trade seriously. The training course included instructions on the use of inks for secret writing, including one preparation codenamed "BS" after its key constituent, birdshit. He was then assigned, "wearing his usual air of indignant bewilderment", to MI6's Iberian section, then run by Kim Philby, which covered Spain, Portugal and their colonies. Muggeridge was despatched to Mozambique, somewhat to the irritation of his section chief, though he returned to London in the latter part of the war, where Philby again enjoyed his "stubborn opposition to the policy of the day (whatever it was)". Never a commited cold warrior, Muggeridge left British Intelligence after the war, with the lesson that

> nothing should ever be done simply if there are devious ways of doing it ... Secrecy is as essential to intelligence as vestments to a mass, or darkness to a spiritual seânce, and must at all costs be maintained, quite irrespective of whether or not it serves any purpose.

Chris MULLIN

Now the Labour MP for Sunderland, Mullin came under MI5 surveillance during the early 1980s. At this time he was a journalist on the leftist monthly *Tribune* and the author of a rather facile novel called *A Very British Coup*, published in 1982, in which a naive but worthy radical Labour Government is subverted and overthrown by nefarious right-wing elements in Whitehall, the City and the CIA. More interesting from MI5's point of view, Mullin was a close associate of left-wing MP Tony *Benn*, who was then engaged in a vigorous campaign to win the deputy leadership of the Labour Party. (In a desperately close battle, Benn was finally defeated by Denis Healey.) At one stage, MI5 acquired a broken recording of a telephone conversation between Mullin and a friend, during which Mullin was apparently discussing Labour defence policy. MI5 immediately concluded that this was part of a new Bennite defence initiative. Only later did they discover that Mullin was actually talking about plots for *A Very British Coup* . . .

Maurice OLDFIELD

Inasmuch as British Intelligence has an image — in Britain, at any rate — it is typified by this diffident, owlish figure. Born in 1915 in the Derbyshire hamlet of Over Hadden, Oldfield trained as an historian and picked up a first-class degree from Manchester University. Like many well-qualified youths of that era, he was recruited into intelligence work during World War II, but whereas most of them returned to civilian careers after 1945, Oldfield's apparent talent for secret work led to his recruitment into the Secret Intelligence Service, MI6, where he remained for nearly the rest of his life.

During World War II, Oldfield was assigned to Security Intelligence Middle East (SIME). This was a kind of regional version of MI5 which was responsible for preventing espionage and "subversion" in British-controlled territories in the Middle East. One of its most successful counter-espionage operations used "double-cross" tactics. The idea was to arrest known German agents, persuade them to work for the British and then use them to feed false or misleading information back to their German controllers, who were hopefully unaware that their erstwhile agents had been turned. Among the double-agents run by Oldfield and his colleagues in SIME were a pair of Greeks code-named QUICKSILVER and PESSIMIST, whom the British kept incommunicado in a villa on the main Beirut-Damascus road. Keeping them happy was not always easy. On one occasion, a furious row erupted between the two agents and a pair of prostitutes sent over to entertain them. The women had insisted that contraceptives be used but "Q and P", as they became known, were furiously indignant. "This is a disgrace," they cried. "It is wrong and insulting and we won't use them. This sort of thing is never done by decent people in Greece."

Oldfield's wartime experience, coupled with the patronage of his immediate superior Brigadier Douglas Roberts, carried him into MI6's counter-espionage section, which in the immediate post-war era was run by none other than Kim Philby. Philby was impressed with Oldfield, describing him in his memoirs as "an officer of high quality" and "formidable", and dubbing him with the nickname "Brig's Brains" — which was rather more charitable than his Foreign Office moniker of "Moulders".

During the 1950s Oldfield served two stints in the MI6 station in Singapore. His work in the Far East, apart from inspiring a penchant for the company of young Asian men, kept him away from the upheavals which engulfed MI6 headquarters after the fall of Philby and the Crabbe fiasco. He also managed to develop good relations with the local CIA operatives which helped to propel him into the senior ranks of MI6 at the turn of the 1960s. He became head of the Washington station from 1960 to 1964. This post, one of the most important in MI6, involved close liaison with the American intelligence complex, particularly the CIA. Relations between the British and American intelligence networks were at an all-time low following Philby's defection, the supposed MI5 "mole" and the split over the Suez crisis. A windfall came Oldfield's way in the form of Oleg Penkovsky, a Soviet colonel who supplied valuable military intelligence during the Cuban missile crisis. However, it was also the heyday of the KGB defector Anatoly *Golitsin*, whose outlandish theories had won over numerous adherents, notably the CIA's influential counter-intelligence boss, James Angleton. Golitsin's claim that Penkovsky was a Soviet plant drew little sympathy from

FREEDOM'S JUST

ANOTHER WORD

Oldfield, who was heard to complain that "the situation here is much more like *Alice in Wonderland* than anything Lewis Carroll could have thought up. There must be several candidates for the role of Mad Hatter."

Oldfield's dry humour was sustained back in London, when he took over the No 2 slot in MI6, as illustrated by an exchange with Labour Minister Dick Crossman in Oldfield's club, the Athenaeum.

"I know all about you MI6 people. You employ a lot of right-wing MPs," Crossman charged.

"Ah, yes, perhaps. But you don't know how many left-wing MPs we may employ," Oldfield countered.

Not everyone was aware of exactly who Oldfield was, although he had been identified in Philby's autobiography as a senior MI6 man ("Why did he name me? I've puzzled about that for a long time," he later opined). Yet confronted with the question which all spooks dread — "What do you do for a living?" — Oldfield would produce the simple, disingenuous answer: "I am head of MI5".

In 1973 Oldfield was appointed Chief of MI6. The agency was, rather against Oldfield's wishes, becoming increasingly involved in the imbroglio of Northern Ireland; and his caution was amply justified by the exposure of the semi-comical MI6-sanctioned exploits of Howard Marks and the Littlejohn brothers. He developed an appreciable fear of the Provisional IRA, who made several attempts to kill him, as well as writing sinister messages ("The IRA will get you") in hymn books at Oldfield's regular church in London. "I have never feared death," he once confided to a friend, "but I don't like the thought of falling into the hands of the IRA, particularly when you see what they do to their own people." Oldfield was not himself unacquainted with the arts of persuasion. Back in the

1950s, a would-be agent remembers him reminiscing at his club about interrogation of Jewish prisoners in Palestine under the British mandate: "Oldfield talked cheerfully about beating them up and pushing people's heads under buckets of water."

Ireland, if not the IRA, did get Oldfield in the end. He left MI6 in 1978 for the sleepy quadrangles of All Souls' College, Oxford, and the pastures of rural Derbyshire. But Margaret Thatcher, who took over as Prime Minister the following year, had not finished with him:

> I was in Derbyshire when the telephone rang. It was the PM's secretary. She asked if I was available to go down to London. I explained that I was just off to Bakewell market with the lads, and my availability would depend on whether I had one or many pints of beer.

Appointment as Northern Ireland Intelligence Coordinator at the end of September 1979 seems to have had a sobering effect on Oldfield. He stopped sending out Christmas cards: "I don't really think I'm in a very Christmassy situation," he confided to a friend. The following June he retired, this time for good. Stricken with cancer, he died in March 1981.

The obituaries concentrated on his alleged similarity to John Le Carré's fictional spymaster George Smiley (and, more improbably, to James Bond's boss "M"). Certainly, there were some points of coincidence, for when Le Carré arranged a first meeting between Oldfield and the actor Alec Guinness, playing Smiley, the latter "nearly blew a gasket watching Oldfield's busy, fat man's waddle. Smiley on the screen and Oldfield were ridiculously similar." Unlike the reserved Smiley, however, Oldfield turned up wearing "disgraceful orange suede boots and with big rings on his hands". Such flamboyance would no doubt have been construed by Oldfield's numerous enemies in Ireland — in MI5 and the security forces as much as the IRA — as evidence of his alleged homosexuality. In 1987, following yet another outraged tome by Chapman Pincher, Prime Minister Thatcher told a shocked House of Commons that a security review, conducted in 1980, concluded that Oldfield was a potential security risk. His security clearance was withdrawn forthwith. The truth is hard to divine. Oldfield's detractors claim that he enjoyed regular "rough trade" and lied during vetting inquiries about his sex life. His supporters contend that his indiscretions were no more than youthful follies and that he was the victim of a smear campaign by MI5, who were supposedly infuriated by the appointment of an intelligence supremo from "the shits across the river" (a reference to MI6 headquarters at Century House, near Waterloo in South London).

Had he ever written an autobiography, Oldfield said that he would have called it "Nothing Worth Nicking". The title derived from the experience of a former colleague who became a prison visitor after retiring from MI6. In conversation one day with a prisoner convicted of burglary, the prisoner disclosed that he once had a job doing repair work on Century House. Naturally enough, the burglar had taken the opportunity to "case the joint", unaware of who occupied the building, but found it rather disappointing.

> Proper rum place it was. People didn't talk to one another in the lifts and they left nothing on their desks. All you need to get into Century House is a ladder and a bag of tools. But it would be a waste of time. Nothing worth nicking there, guv'nor.

THE SECRET LIFE OF ALFRED, LORD TENNYSON

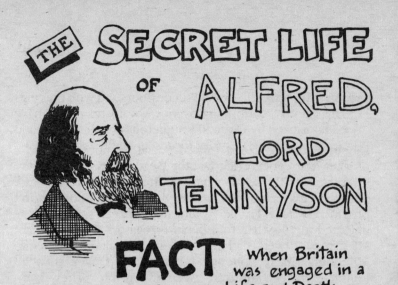

FACT When Britain was engaged in a Life and Death struggle with **RUSSIA** this soi-disant "poet" churned out doggerel in an attempt to undermine morale among the British troops. His "Charge of the Light Brigade" contains the scurrilous slander that the British generals were incompetent — "Someone had blundered..."

FACT Tennyson, when a student at Cambridge, was a member of the "Apostles". It is surely not without significance that other members of this society included Anthony Blunt and Guy Burgess.

FACT There is no record anywhere that Tennyson ever denied membership of the Communist Party.

FACT

David OWEN

Labour Party whizz-kid turned Social Democrat mould-breaker, the egocentric "Doctor Death" was at one time fingered by MI5 as an agent of the Czech intelligence service. This erroneous notion arose from information provided by Josef Frolik, a Major in the Czech service who defected in 1969. He told his interrogators that a Labour MP named "Owen" had been passing information to them. MI5 immediately concluded that David Owen, then a junior Defence Minister, was responsible. They had forgotten that the Labour back benches sported another MP of that name — Will Owen, the ageing member for Morpeth in Northumberland, who was the real culprit.

Later, however, Will Owen was duly charged under the Official Secrets Act and tried in May 1970. Although he admitted supplying information to the Czechs in exchange for money he was acquitted on the novel premise that none of the information was classified, a point which MI5 had somehow overlooked. Despite the acquittal, MI5 were unconvinced: they asked Leo Abse, a parliamentary colleague, to persuade Owen to submit to further questioning. Owen agreed, subject to a guarantee of immunity. As he accompanied Owen to the interrogation, Abse's abiding memory of MI5 was the "00" prefix to the numbers on each office. "I was disappointed that our destined room did not prove to be '007'," he recalls.

Tommy ROBERTS

Civil servant. Head of information at Stormont under Roy Mason, the Northern Ireland Secretary in the 1976-79 Callaghan Government. At a party thrown by the Northern Ireland Office, Roberts fell into conversation with *Guardian* journalist Anne McHardy and started to discuss a recent argument between her and her husband. Asked how he knew about it, Roberts said he had listened to tapes from a tap on McHardy's phone. "I asked him to repeat the story again and, luckily for me, he was drunk enough to do it," she said.

Bertrand RUSSELL

The renowned philosopher incurred MI5's displeasure during the 1960s for his leading role in the Committee of 100, a peace group which advocated non-violent direct action against the state's nuclear infrastructure. Russell and his fellow activists are credited with pioneering the technique of organising fake events — meetings, pickets or demonstrations — over the telephone, in the knowledge that some of the conversations would be monitored by the security services and the "intelligence" passed on to the police. Committee of 100 members would then record the presence of large numbers of police standing around twiddling their thumbs at the site of non-existent events.

This tactic has since been used on numerous occasions, particularly in the course of industrial disputes. On one occasion during the 1980 steelworkers' strike, union organisers arranged an imaginary mass picket at the improbable venue of Rosselli's ice-cream factory in Rotherham. Yet within just four minutes a police car and two vans arrived, expecting no doubt to find brawny steelmen wrestling in the street with ice-cream van drivers. The factory gates were, of course, completely deserted and remained that way, much to the chagrin of the police and the amusement of the watching strike committee.

Arthur SCARGILL

Left-wing leader of the mineworkers' union and a regular target of MI5 surveillance. According to a former MI5 transcription clerk, Scargill "would occasionally shout abuse at the people who were tapping him".

Now look here, Funereal-Jerque! You were at Eton. You got a first-class degree at Oxford. You served in the Guards.

Yet your very first operation for MI5..... and you fail completely!

All you had to do was go to Belfast and tap a few phones.....

Perhaps the equipment was faulty....?

The equipment was perfect, old boy.....

...I simply could not understand that appalling accent....

Bernard SHELDON

Known to British newspapers as Bernard X, Sheldon is shortly due to retire from his long-standing post as MI5's legal adviser. His enigmatically truncated surname is the result of Government requests to the media that his real name should not be published. Interest in Sheldon arose from his intimate involvement in the Peter Wright affair. Indeed, it is believed in some quarters that the various decisions to pursue Wright through the courts of the world have been taken by Thatcher, advised by Sheldon, and have nothing to do with the Attorney-General (until recently Sir Michael Havers) who is formally responsible for such decisions and as such carries the can. However, it is also possible that Thatcher has confused Sheldon with Norman Tebbit, to whom he bears a physical likeness. Sheldon may have mixed feelings about his role in the Wright imbroglio: the pair were regular drinking partners once upon a time and could often be seen, accompanied by a burly minder, frequenting hostelries near MI5's Counter-Espionage Branch headquarters near Euston station.

Michael SHELDON

A sometime student at the Joint Services Language School, a now-defunct establishment based in Cambridge where squaddies were taught Russian and other languages, often in preparation for signals intelligence work. At one stage during the course, an officer informed his class that they would have to sign the Official Secrets Act. The ceremony, conducted with due solemnity, took place in a classroom full of electrical equipment. At the end of the proceedings a technician clad in overalls crawled out from underneath one of the benches. He had clearly been present throughout and the presiding officer, realising that a breach of security had occurred, promptly had him arrested and taken away under guard. In the late 1960s MI5 came to the conclusion that the school was a prime recruiting ground for the Soviet KGB and had it closed down as a security risk, but it is not clear whether the technician was in fact a Russian agent.

Max SCHULTZ

One of MI5's earliest successes was the capture and conviction in 1911 of this German spy. Schultz, a Doctor of Philosophy, made his base in a houseboat near Plymouth where he gave a number of parties, hoping to induce some unsuspecting guest to divulge secrets of His Majesty's navy. His insistence on flying the German flag on the mast of his boat, however, gave him something less than perfect cover. After a brief investigation, MI5 decided to have him arrested. As the joint MI5-police team approached the houseboat, they observed a suspected agent of Schultz's coming from the opposite direction. Fearing that he should arrive before them and inform Schultz of their presence, the spycatchers inventively diverted a flock of sheep across the path. The suspect, a local solicitor called Duff, "got thoroughly mixed up with them . . . careering one way and then the other". MI5 arrived first and found Schultz with enough incriminating material to have him hauled in. At his trial, he was charged as (Doctor) Phil Max Schultz: the court clerks had not realised that "Phil" referred to Doctor of Philosophy and put it down as a Christian name.

Jim SKARDON

An ex-policeman who became MI5's chief interrogator immediately after World War II. His successes with atom-bomb spy Klaus Fuchs and others earned him promotion to head of the "Watchers" section which carried out physical surveillance; following Russian diplomats and spy suspects on foot and in cars. Skardon was most insistent that each car have three men (the Watchers didn't employ women at that time for reasons of propriety). "There's one to drive, one to read the map, and the third to operate the radio." The Watcher vehicles were not always as inconspicuous as they might have hoped: on one occasion, a Watcher vehicle was spotted because it had recently changed its number plates — or rather, *one* of its number plates.

After his retirement, Skardon refused a £100,000 offer to write his memoirs because his former bosses wouldn't like it. And despite his sterling services to security, he was aware of the endemic paranoia within MI5 produced by the mole-hunt of the 1960s and '70s: "They'll probably wait until I'm dead and then announce that I was the eighth man".

I was once a member of an obscure socialist organisation.

One day I realised that our group had been penetrated. There was a spy——a goverment agent—in our midst!

A hastily convened ad hoc sub-committee quickly identified the guilty party and it was resolved to expel him.

But we didn't. After all he had a car and he was clearly the most hard-working and dedicated activist in our group....

Howard SMITH

Previously a career diplomat and ambassador to the Soviet Union, Smith was made Director-General of MI5 in 1978. The appointment, which marked yet another attempt to "clean up" the service, was much resented within MI5 who dislike outside intruders at any level, let alone the top. It later transpired that at an embassy reception held shortly before his departure from Moscow, Smith had actually told the Soviet Prime Minister, Alexei Kosygin, that he was the new head of MI5. Despite this flagrant breach of the Official Secrets Act, Smith was not prosecuted and remained in his spy job until 1981.

Ronnie STONEHAM

The MI5 link-man at the BBC inhabits Room 105 of Broadcasting House — the reputed model for Orwell's "Ministry of Truth" — where he works under the guise "Sp A to D Pers" (Special Assistant to Director of Personnel). His job is weeding out "subversives" from the Beeb's staff by checking their personal details against MI5's half-million strong names index. Inside the BBC this process is known mysteriously as "colleging". Anyone unfortunate enough to come to Stoneham's attention has their personnel department file stamped with a special

symbol resembling a Christmas tree.

Some months after Stoneham and his works were comprehensively blown by the *Observer* in the summer of 1985, he received a peculiar visit from a gang of BBC journalists. While preparing a background piece on the trial of eight Royal Signals squaddies in the Cyprus sex-for-secrets case, they had discovered that Stoneham was a former Signals Officer and chaired the Royal Corps of Signals Welfare Association. Using the us-Beeb-chaps-should-all-help-each-other argument, the hacks tried to solicit his asistance in compiling this piece. Stoneham was furious. "This is outrageous. My allegiance is to the Crown!" he cried, before throwing them out.

Basil THOMSON

Perhaps the most famous head of the police Special Branch in its century-long history was Basil Thomson, who held the job between 1913 and 1921. The son of an archbishop, Thomson had earlier enjoyed an unorthodox career as Prime Minister of Tonga, personal tutor to the Crown Prince of Siam and Governor of Dartmoor prison. His encounters with the indigenous peoples of the Pacific made a strong impression on him.

> My first native friends were cannibals, but I learned very quickly that the warrior who had eaten his man as a quasi-religious act was a far more estimable person than the town-bred, mission-educated native.

By the time Thomson took over at the Branch, the early threats from Fenian bombers and anarchists had subsided.

Nonetheless, Thomson perceived abundant subversive potential in anti-war groups, the labour movement and the media. Among his early coups was the suppression of the *Globe* newspaper which in 1915 reported (erroneously) that the British Commander-in-Chief, Lord Kitchener, had resigned. Thomson went down to the *Globe* offices and spoke to the print-shop foreman.

> "Supposing you wanted to take away some part of this machinery which would make it impossible to run the machines again until it was restored and yet do no damage to the plant, what would you take?"

> "Oh, that's easy," replied the foreman, and he lead me to a certain engine from which he took a portion which I could carry away in my hand. I thanked him and carried it away. That was how the *Globe* was suppressed until such time as the directors had come to an arrangement with the Government.

After the Russian revolution of 1917, Thomson promulgated a doom-laden vision of Bolshevik-inspired workers' revolts throughout Britain. His analysis was eagerly swallowed by the Government who gave him a virtual carte blanche to spy on the labour movement and political activists. Thomson's assessment was undoubtedly affected by his discovery that Bolshevism was not a political philosophy but

> an infectious disease, spreading rapidly, but insidiously, until like a cancer it eats away the fabric of society, and the patient ceases even to wish for his own recovery. A nation attacked by it may . . . be reduced to a political and social morass . . . while civilisation crumbles away and the country returns to its original barbarism.

It was not long, however, before Thomson discovered the communist view that "the British public is far too sunk

" THE MAIN THING IS TO MAKE SURE THAT THE PUBLIC DON'T GET TO HEAR ABOUT IT … "

in apathy and acquiescence with its conditions of slavery to capitalism to make it worthwhile . . . attempting to convert it to the gospel of revolution". Nevertheless, fear of the Russians, coupled with Thomson's dynamic self-importance, meant that there was no relaxation in the surveillance of subversive elements. The Russian angle brought Thomson into conflict with Vernon Kell, his opposite number at MI5, over who should be snooping on whom. Thomson had stronger support in the Government but Kell was the better bureaucratic tactician. In 1921, MI5 took charge of both spy-catching and watching subversives. Thomson was forcibly pensioned off.

Thomson spent his retirement turning out volumes of memoirs and detective stories. His last actual contact with the police took place in December 1925, when he was arrested in Hyde Park in the company of a Miss Thelma de Lava and charged with violating public decency. Although he was convicted and fined five pounds, rumours abounded that Sir Basil, as he became, had been framed by Whitehall enemies or by subversives.

Bridie and Tim WALLIS

It seems that MI5 and Special Branch have recently hit upon a bizarre technique for procuring the identities and phone numbers of people who telephone subversive individuals. (For technical reasons, it is not easy for the phone-tappers to locate the source of incoming calls to a telephone which they are monitoring.) The only problem is that the victims will almost inevitably find out about it, as the example of Tim and Bridie Wallis showed.

During 1985 the Wallis couple lived next door to a proposed Cruise missile base at Molesworth in Cambridgeshire. They are Quakers, and at the time were active in the local peace movement. Their home became a convenient contact point for anti-missile campaigners, which rendered them likely targets for surveillance by the security services. One of the Wallis's experiences with their telephone was bizarre even by the standards of strange telephone stories which emanate from paranoid peaceniks.

In February that year, a major demonstration was planned outside the Molesworth base. On 31 January, a fellow campaigner phoned the Wallis home. After obtaining first an engaged tone, then the unobtainable tone, the caller was connected to an answering machine, from which the following message was delivered.

> This is Tim and Bridie Wallis's number. We are out at the moment. Please leave your name, address and phone number and we will ring you back.

The voice — male, with a slight American accent — was a passable imitation of Tim Wallis's. Later on, the caller mentioned the incident to the Wallises. They were puzzled. They didn't have an answering machine.

When the incident was raised in the House of Commons at the end of February, Home Secretary Leon Brittan replied with the customary formula of "it is not the practice to comment on individual cases". This immediately drew a fifth-form interruption from the veteran Tory backbencher Sir Anthony Kershaw:

> Is my right honourable and learned Friend aware that if he is not watching these people, I want my money back?

To which Brittan replied:
  Without going, as is customary, any further into these details, I can only say that my honourable Friend should not expect a refund.
The obvious solution to Kershaw's demand is to privatise MI5. In this way, shareholders who don't like its choice of surveillance targets can vote with their cheque-books.

Nigel WEST

"Nigel West" is the writing pseudonym of Rupert Allason, the newly elected Conservative MP for Torbay in Devon and the author of a gaggle of books on various aspects of the British intelligence complex, all of which have been published since 1980. The purpose of the pen-name, he told the *Observer* in 1987, is to protect him from accusations of exploiting family connections — a puzzling line of reasoning since his identity has been well-known since his first book appeared. His father was also a Conservative MP; his wife is Nicky Oppenheimer, heiress to the eponymous diamond fortune.

Allason entered the spy-hack milieu after landing a researcher's job in the late 1970s on an encyclopaedia of espionage. He then worked with another espionage writer, Donald McCormick (who calls himself "Richard Deacon"), on the BBC documentary series "Spy!" before branching out on his own. His first two books on MI5's work before and after 1945 are remarkable for their sheer volume of detail — "like going through MI5's filing cabinets", in the words of historian Anthony Glees (real name) — and the paucity of their analysis. His more recent efforts have drawn less complimentary notices. A 1986 book on GCHQ drew a caustic conclusion from ex-employee Alex Hamilton:

> Given the newsworthiness of GCHQ, many people will be tempted to buy this awful book. At least the many howlers should provoke some mirth, and perhaps a sigh of relief in some quarters . . . . An awful book, yes, but I doubt if anyone will write a better one.

Allason's most recent work, published shortly before his election to Parliament, returns to his familiar theme of moles in MI5. It wasn't Hollis, says "West", it was his deputy, Mitchell. On this occasion, the major challenge to his theory comes from fellow author Chapman Pincher (close to real name: Harry Pincher) who insists that Hollis was the bad 'un.

Allason is 35 while Pincher is 73, but the pair have much professional common ground. Both share the same right-wing politics, the same mildly sychopantic interest in MI5 (especially the mole saga), the same sort of contacts (disaffected ex-MI5 officers), the same tolerance and discreet assistance from officialdom, and the same talent for self-publicity. Not surprisingly, they loathe each other.

The opening salvo in the seven years' war of mutual abuse was a volley from Pincher in a sniffy *Daily Express* review of the first Nigel West book, *MI5: British Security Service Operations 1909-45*.

> Mr West claims he has had much official help but I can find no security or intelligence officer who has heard of him. In his marginal references to really sensitive issues such as the Hollis Affair, Mr West is either uninformed or has had the wool pulled over his eyes.

For good measure, Pincher revealed West's true identity.

In his next book, Allason struck a neat counter-blow with a story about Pincher. In 1961, Pincher reported to Rear-Admiral George Thomson, Secretary to the D Notice Committee , that he had established "an important contact" on the Soviet embassy staff and would be willing to help MI5 with information. After some internal argument, Pincher was invited for an interview with an MI5 case officer. Both parties were initially satisfied: Pincher thought he had been recruited as a secret agent, while MI5 believed that he might actually have a useful contact. West concludes:

> Pincher spun out his link with [MI5] but it became obvious that there was no possible advantage to retaining him as a "window" into the Soviet camp and he was given a gentle brush-off.

Pincher would surely have been riled by such public humiliation. He refrains from discussing West on the record with outsiders, but his opinions are apparent from correspondence which has found its way into the public domain. Comments such as "people like West who have only superficial knowledge of what went on . . . ." are typical.

West is less forthright but more acidic. "As a ghost-writer in the 1960s style, he has very considerable talents," he says of Pincher in reference to the Pincher-Wright collaboration on *Their Trade Is Treachery*.

More intriguing than the bitching with Pincher is the nature of West's relations with the Government. *A Matter of Trust: MI5 1945-72* played a key part in wrecking the Government's chance of getting an injunction in Australia to stop publication of Peter Wright's *Spycatcher*. The reason, in essence, was that it contained detailed information supplied by former MI5 personnel. Not only did the

Government know that in advance, but officials agreed deletions in West's original draft which left much of this information intact. In effect, publication of *A Matter of Trust* was authorised: the Government's initial submission to the court, which denied authorisation, was dismissed by the judge as "unacceptable". Crucially, by letting the book go ahead, HM Government had connived in precisely the sort of breach of confidence to which they objected so vehemently in the case of *Spycatcher*.

The *Guardian* unwisely suggested that the failure to take an action against Allason over *A Matter of Trust* was a consequence of his Tory Party connections — he boasts friendship with Norman Tebbit among others — an insinuation which cost the newspaper an out-of-court charitable donation. As for suggestions that his books are sponsored or commissioned by the Government, Allason "howls with laughter". "I can categorically deny ever having been spoon-fed material by the Government, the security service or any official source," he adds. Nonetheless, Allason is uniquely privileged in securing Government consent to reveal classified information from inside the intelligence complex: with such beneficience, who needs sponsorship? Perhaps Allason's secret lies in his attitude, which is sharply different from that of his arch-rival. Whereas Pincher likes to see himself as the scourge of Whitehall, Allason candidly admits to being tame. "My loyalty is not to the media. I know it sounds pompous, but it is to the country — what I would call the national interest."

Adolphus WILLIAMSON

Commonly known as "Dolly", Williamson was appointed the first head of the Metropolitan Police "Special Irish Branch" in March 1883 during the Fenian bombing campaign of that era. "Dolly" was an experienced detective who felt strongly about the hardships suffered by himself and his colleagues in the course of their work. In 1880 he wrote:

> the uncertainty and irregularity of the duties (are) . . . . in many cases very distasteful and repugnant to the better class of men in the service, as their duties constantly bring them into contact with the worst classes, frequently cause unnecessary drinking, and compel them at times to resort to trickey [sic] practices which they dislike.

"Dolly" and his Branch suffered an embarrassing setback the year after their formation. After receipt of a threatening letter of apparently Fenian origin, a constable was instructed to patrol around the Metropolitan Police headquarters in Great Scotland Yard and to keep an eye out for suspicious persons and objects. On 30 May 1884, he carried out his normal duties which included a search of the public lavatory directly underneath the Yard. Somehow he failed to detect a large bomb which had been planted there. When the device went off in the early evening a large part of the premises was destroyed, including the Branch offices on the first floor. A frantic search of other suspect conveniences ensued: one near Windsor Castle, occasional residence of the Royal Family, was closed down. The biggest panic, however, followed the discovery that the House of Commons' plumbing was being overhauled by Irish workers.

David WOOD

Formerly the political editor of the *Times*, Wood was apparently unable to cope with the existence of the intelligence establishment. In 1971 he wrote:

> We all both want the secret police and hate having them. But it is a necessary evil, and the thought of it is better forgotten or wished away if we are not to be hypocrites.

Peter WRIGHT

"The wilderness of mirrors, where defectors are false, lies are truth, truth lies and the reflections leave you dazzled and confused": this now-famous phrase was coined by James Jesus Angleton, the CIA's long-serving head of Counter-Intelligence, who became a quasi-mentor to Peter Wright and shared his obsession with the seemingly labyrinthine weavings of Soviet Intelligence. Wright had joined MI5 from Marconi after doing some contract work on a new Soviet bugging device in the early 1950s. MI5's technical prowess, he discovered, was minimal. Through adroit use of radio and electronic surveillance equipment, ably assisted by a few trusty sidekicks, Wright forced his way into the mainstream of MI5. His analyses of the scale and sophistication of Soviet intelligence operations, based on new-fangled methods including complex studies of radio traffic patterns, ran against the grain of traditional MI5 thinking and into the opposition of other MI5 officers, including his superiors. Wright interpreted their stance as derived variously from ignorance and inertia; later on, bolstered by an Angletonesque theoretical framework, he put it down to obstruction by a Soviet agent within the security service.

Culturally, as Wright never tires of repeating, he was poles apart from the effete, upper-middle-class types who dominated MI5's higher echelons. In the early years of his career, he found that

> the atmosphere reminded me of a minor public school. The Directors [of MI5's six branches] were treated with that mixture of reverence and sycophancy reserved by schoolboys for their schoolmasters, and section heads were their prefects.

Most of them "wouldn't have known a bug if it bit them" (to quote John McWilliam MP in a different context). Much of their time was spent at Lords watching cricket or lounging around in their Leconfield House offices doing the *Times* crossword. Thus Peter and his best chums Hugh (Winterborn) and Leslie (Jagger) — who had some wizard lock-picking gear — decided to pull a few japes on the Russians and their mysterious secret society — the KGB. After some of the japes went wrong, it gradually dawned on Peter and his chums that somebody was telling the Russians what they were up to. Not only that, it seemed that the KGB were stealing things from the school tuck shop. Some of the other pupils agreed, including Arthur (Martin) and a prefect named Furnival-Jones whom everybody called FJ. Arthur and Peter soon became chums and vowed to find out who was sneaking on them. Suspicion focussed on the quirky Mr Mitchell, the deputy headmaster, who was a compulsive toothpick user, and subsequently the headmaster himself, the sinister Mr

Hollis, who had been to China . . . .

What followed was a manic mole-hunt inside MI5 as Wright, Martin and company turned the service upside down and inside out throughout the 1960s and either side thereof. The search was inconclusive. Wright sets out his evidence in *Spycatcher*, with the help of ghost-writer Paul Greengrass of Granada TV, at great and often tedious length. Much of the evidence in the book is indeterminate to the point where it should be possible to conclude (a) that Wright himself was the mole, or (b) that there was no mole. The inevitable result of all this hunting was that the rest of MI5 got thoroughly sick of Wright and Martin and gradually squeezed them out.

Martin was immediately taken on by the counter-intelligence section of MI6, the foreign intelligence service for which Wright reserves nearly as much venom as the management of his own outfit. Whereas, during the mid-1950s for example, MI5 technical operations were "highly professional", the Broadway mafia would "never settle for a disaster if calamity could be found instead". Higher up the pyramid, in the misty realms of the Cabinet Office, the clubby claustrophobia of the intelligence mandarinate resembled not so much a public school as "a small village in the Home Counties".

Wright himself eventually rose to become a "prefect" as head of D3, the counter-espionage research section. In this job, he reports:

> I did suggest examining the possibilities of planting booby trapped detonators on the Provisionals. It would have been a feasible operation in conjunction with MI6, along the same lines as the Cyprus plan to plant fake receivers on Grivas. But even the MI5 management took fright, and refused to investigate the

plan any further.

"That's murder," I was told.

"Innocent people are being killed and maimed every day," I said. "Which policy do you think the British people would like us to pursue?"

Nevertheless, despite his rise to this position — earned, it seems, through his manifest talents as an intelligence functionary — he could never quite come to terms with the system in which he operated. With a few exceptions, he despised his colleagues, many of whom, he noted, needed psychiatric counselling "to assist them in carrying the burdens of secrecy". The common sentiment in the offices, according to Wright, is that "the fun has gone". And if the head of MI5 was a Soviet agent, well, it could have been worse: he could have been in CND.

Courtney YOUNG

Head of Soviet Counter-Espionage in the 1950s and undisputed MI5 crossword king. Each morning most of MI5's senior staff settled down to the *Times* crossword. After a short while strange coded messages wafted over the scrambled internal phone system such as "My left rump is giving me trouble" or "My right breast is vacant" meaning, respectively, "What is 7 down in the bottom left-hand corner?" and "What's 12 across in the middle?"

Victor ZAKIN

Naval Attaché at the Soviet embassy in March 1985, the time of Cathy Massiter's televised disclosures of MI5 naughty business. The broadcasting of this film was held up for a fortnight by the Independent Broadcasting Authority, who feared prosecution under the Official Secrets Act. In the meantime Twenty-Twenty Vision, the production company which made the film, started selling videotape copies to the public. Zakin duly appeared in the company's London offices. "I want to see the banned programme, so give me the famous cassette," he announced. One of the staff asked who he was. "My name is Victor Zakin. And I live at 23 Campden Hill Gardens. Now give me the famous cassette."

DOING THE DOUBLE

A country road.

A tree.

Two former MI5 employees are waiting....

For some strange reason they have Russian names....

Vladivar: Is this the right place?

Smirnoff: I can't answer that question. The Official Secrets Act ....

Vladivar: Are you sure it's today...

Smirnoff: I'm sorry... The Official Secrets Act, you know.

Vladivar: I'm beginning to suspect that I'm in the wrong play .... (Smirnoff does not respond) .... Let's go and see a James Bond film.

Smirnoff: All right. We'll go now.
                    (They do not move)